D0916035

1 9 9 9 - 0 0

STAR GUIDE™

1999-00

STAR GUIDE™

Published by:

Axiom Information Resources

Ann Arbor, Michigan 48107

1999-2000 STAR GUIDE™
Published by Axiom Information Resources
Ann Arbor, Michigan 48107 USA

Copyright ©1999 Axiom Information Resources

All rights reserved. No part of this publication
may be reproduced or distributed in any form or
by any means, or stored in a data base or retrieval
system, without the prior written permission of
the publishers.

Published by:
Axiom Information Resources
P.O. Box 8015
Ann Arbor, MI 48107

Printed in USA
ISBN # 0-943213-30-4
ISSN # 1060-9997

Cover Design by: Concialdi Design

SPECIAL SALES
The 1999-2000 STAR GUIDE™ is
available at special quantity discounts
for bulk purchases. For information write:

Axiom Information Resources
P.O. Box 8015-TX
Ann Arbor, MI 48107

Contents

Order Blanks and Customer Response Form (See Back Page)

INTRODUCTION

The aim of Star Guide™ 1999-2000 is to provide a complete list that acknowledges today's stars in all fields of human accomplishment along with their most accurate, up-to-date address. The universe of stars—a universe as diverse as Oprah Winfrey, Candice Bergen, Jerry Seinfeld, Zubin Mehta, Tom Hanks, Roseanne as well as Rupaul—is completely indexed, and alphabetically arranged under five convenient categories: Movie and TV, Music, Sports, Politics, and Other Famous People.

Star Guide™ 1999-2000 is a valuable communications tool that allows you and the stars to enjoy the human contact which is not possible through a star's performance or activity. With the Star Guide™, your favorite star can receive your praise, reassurance, criticism or offer of help. In return, stars often provide thanks, encouragement, recommendations, photos, autographs or other tokens of appreciation.

More than just a tool for the ordinary fan, the Star Guide™ is an invaluable resource tool for the reference librarian, collector, fund-raiser, trivia buff or anyone with any reason to contact a person of prominence.

Every reasonable effort has been made to ensure accurate addresses at press time, but stars obviously may move or change the circumstance by which they receive mail. Therefore, we cannot accept responsibility for inaccurate addresses. If there's a star you think should be listed but isn't write to us, and we'll try to include them in the next edition. Please remember, when writing to Axiom Information Resources, as well as when writing your favorite star, it is always best to enclose a self-addressed, stamped envelope. Please send your comments to Axiom Information Resources, P.O. Box 8015, Ann Arbor, MI 48107.

Star Guide's 1999-2000 Stars of the Year:

Movie.......... Antonio Banderas
Television.... Oprah Winfrey
Music.......... Boyz II Men
Sports.......... Tiger Woods
Politics....... Bill Clinton
Others......... Diana, Princess of Wales

(Please send us your star's of the year to the address above)

Movies/TV

They're Not A Star Until
They're A Star In Star Guide™

A _____ A

Dihanne Abbott
460 West Avenue #46
Los Angeles, CA 90065

Ian Abercrombie
1040 N. Gardner
Los Angeles, CA 90046

F. Murray Abraham
40 Fifth Avenue #2C
New York, NY 10011

Victoria Abril
11 rue Chanez
F-75016, Paris, France

Ray Abruzzo
20334 Pacific Coast Hwy.
Malibu, CA 90265

Leslie Ackerman
4439 Worster Avenue
Studio City, CA 91604

Jay Acovone
3811 Multiview Drive
Los Angeles, CA 90068

Brooke Adams
248 S. Van Ness Avenue
Los Angeles, CA 90004

Cindy Adams
1050 Fifth Avenue
New York, NY 10028

Mason Adams
900 - 5th Avenue
New York, NY 10021

Maud Adams
11901 Sunset Blvd. #214
Los Angeles, CA 90049

Isabelle Adjani
2 rue Lord Byron
F-75008, Paris, FRANCE

John Agar
639 N. Hollywood Way
Burbank, CA 91505

Ben Affleck
639 N. Hollywood Way
Burbank, CA 91505

John Agar
639 N. Hollywood Way
Burbank, CA 91505

Jenny Agutter
1026 Montana Avenue
Santa Monica, CA 90403

Danny Aiello
4 Thornhill Drive
Ramsey, NJ 07446

Anouk Aimee
201 rue du Faubourg Street
Honore, F-75008 Paris FRANCE

Eddie Albert
719 Amalfi Drive
Pacific Palisades, CA 90272

Edward Albert
27320 Winding Way
Malibu, CA 90265

Dolores Albin
23388 Mulholland Drive
Woodland Hills, CA 91364

Alan Alda
641 Lexington Avenue #1400
New York, NY 10022

Frank Aletter
5430 Corbin Avenue
Tarzana, CA 91356

Denise Alexander
270 N. Canon Drive #1199
Beverly Hills, CA 90210

Jason Alexander
405 S. Beverly Drive #500
Beverly Hills, CA 90210

Kristian Alfonso
P.O. Box 557
Brockton, MA 02403

Tatyana Ali
4924 Balboa Blvd. #377
Encino, CA 91316

Jed Allan
P.O. Box 5302
Blue Jay, CA 92317

Chad Allen
6489 Cavalleri Road #204
Malibu, CA 90265

Elizabeth Allen
P.O. Box 243
Lake Peekskill, NY 10537

Jonelle Allen
8730 Sunset Blvd. #480
Los Angeles, CA 90069

Sean Barbara Allen
1622 Sierra Bonita Avenue
Los Angeles, CA 90046

Steve Allen
15201-B Burbank Blvd.
Van Nuys, CA 91411

Tim Allen
1122 S. Robertson Blvd. #15
Los Angeles, CA 90035

Woody Allen
930 Fifth Avenue
New York, NY 10018

Kirstie Alley
132 S. Rodeo Drive #300
Beverly Hills, CA 90212

Christopher Allport
121 N. San Vincente Blvd.
Beverly Hills, CA 90211

June Allyson
1651 Foothill Road
Ojai, CA 93020

Maria Conchita Alonso
P.O. Box 537
Beverly Hills, CA 90213

Carol Alt
111 East 22nd Street #200
New York, NY 10010

Jeff Altman
5065 Calvin Avenue
Tarzana, CA 91356

Trini Alvarado
233 Park Avenue So. 10th Flr.
New York, NY 10003

Ana-Alicia
1148 4th Street #206
Santa Monica, CA 90403

Barbara Anderson
P.O. Box 10118
Santa Fe, NM 87504

Gillian Anderson
110-555 Brooks Bank Avenue, #10
No. Vancouver B.C. V7J 3S5
CANADA

Loni Anderson
3355 Clerendon Road
Beverly Hills, CA 90210

Melissa Sue Anderson
1558 Will Geer Road
Topanga, CA 90290

Michael J. Anderson
3838 Vinton Avenue #302
Culver City, CA 90232

Melody Anderson
1640 S. Sepulveda Blvd. #218
Los Angeles, CA 90025

Pamela Anderson-Lee
9255 Sunset Blvd. #920
Los Angeles, CA 90069

Richard Anderson
10120 Cielo Drive
Beverely Hills, CA 90210

Bibi Andersson
Tykovagen 28
Lidingo 18161 SWEDEN

Ursula Andress
Via F. Siaci 38
I-00197 Rome ITALY

Anthony Andrews
Unit 5/3-4, The Chambers
Chelsea Harbour
London SW10 OFX ENGLAND

Tige Andrews
4914 Encino Terrace
Encino, CA 91316

Vanessa Angels
9000 Sunset Blvd. #1200
Los Angeles, CA 90069

Jennifer Aniston
5750 Wilshire Blvd. #580
Los Angeles, CA 90036

Michael Ansara
4624 Park Mirasol
Calabasas, CA 91302

Susan Anspach
473 16th Street
Santa Monica, CA 90402

Lysette Anthony
25-22 Marshall Street #300
London WIV 1LL England

Susan Anton
16830 Ventura Blvd. #300
Encino, CA 91436

Gabrielle Anwar
253-26th Street #A-203
Santa Monica, CA 90402

Christina Applegate
9055 Hollywood Hills Road
Los Angeles, CA 90046

Carmen Argenziano
753 Kemp Street
Burbank, CA 91505

Adam Arkin
2372 Veteran Avenue #102
Los Angeles, CA 90064

Curtis Armstrong
3867 Shannon Road
Los Angeles, CA 90027

Lucie Arnaz
P.O. Box 636
Cross River, NY 10518

James Arness
P.O. Box 49003
Los Angeles, CA 90049

Tom Arnold
638 Lindero Canyon Road #367
Agoura Hills, CA 91301

Patricia Arquette
9560 Wilshire Blvd. #516
Beverly Hills, CA 90212

Rosanna Arquette
7704 Woodrow Wilson Drive
Los Angeles, CA 90046

Beatrice Arthur
2000 Old Ranch Road
Los Angeles, CA 90049

Linden Ashby
12424 Wilshire Blvd. #840
Los Angeles, CA 90025

Jane Asher
Coventry Street
London W1 ENGLAND

Elizabeth Ashley
1223 N. Ogden Drive
Los Angeles, CA 90046

Jennifer Ashley
11130 Huston Street #6
Hollywood, CA 91601

Edward Asner
12400 Ventura Blvd., #371
Studio City, CA 91604

Jennifer Aspen
10390 Santa Monica Blvd. #300
Los Angeles, CA 90025

Armand Assante
367 Windsor Highway
New Windsor, NY 12553

John Astin
P.O. Box 49698
Los Angeles, CA 90049

Sean Astin
5438 Norwich Avenue
Van Nuys, CA 91411

Christopher Atkins
6934 Bevis Avenue
Van Nuys, CA 91405

Rene Auberjonois
8428-C Melrose Place
Los Angeles, CA 90069

Nadja Auermann
Via San Vittore 40
I-20123 Milan ITALY

Claudine Auger
151 El Camino Drive
Beverly Hills, CA 90212

Karen Austin
3356 Rowena Avenue
Los Angeles, CA 90027

Dan Aykroyd
1180 S. Beverly Blvd. #618
Los Angeles, CA 90035

Hank Azaria
2211 Corinth #210
Los Angeles, CA 90064

Candice Azzara
8899 Beverly Blvd., #510
Los Angeles, CA 90048

B   **B**

Lauren Bacall
1 W. 72nd Street #43
New York, NY 10023

Barbara Bain
1501 Skylark Lane
W. Hollywood, CA 90069

Scott Baio
4333 Forman Avenue
Toluca Lake, CA 91602

Scott Bairstow
9701 Wilshire Blvd., 10th Floor
Beverly Hills, CA 90212

Joe Don Baker
23339 Hatteras
Woodland Hills, CA 91364

Tyler Baker
4731 Laurel Canyon Blvd. #200
North Hollywood, CA 91607

Brenda Bakke
21838 Encina Road
Topanga, CA 90290

Alec Baldwin
132 S. Rodeo Drive #300
Beverly Hills, CA 90212

William Baldwin
955 S. Carrillo Drive #200
Los Angeles, CA 90048

Paula Barbieri
P.O. Box 20483
Panama City, FL 32411

Brigitte Bardot
F-83990 La Madrigue
St. Tropez, FRANCE

Bob Barker
1851 Outpost Drive
Los Angeles, CA 90068

Ellen Barkin
9830 Wilshire Blvd.
Beverly Hills, CA 90212

Priscilla Barnes
8428-C Melrose Place
W. Hollywood, CA 90069

Majel Barrett
P.O. Box 691370
W. Hollywood, CA 90069

Drew Barrymore
1122 South Robertson Blvd. #15
Los Angeles, CA 90035

Kim Basinger
4833 Don Juan Place
Woodland Hills, CA 91367

Angela Bassett
9911 W. Pico Blvd. PH #1
Los Angeles, CA 90035

Amelia Batchelor
14811 Mulholland Drive
Los Angeles, CA 90024

Jason Bateman
2623 - 2nd Street
Santa Monica, CA 90405

Justine Bateman
11288 Ventura Blvd. #190
Studio City, CA 91604

Alan Bates
122 Hamilton Terrace
London NW8 9UT ENGLAND

Kathy Bates
6220 Del Valle
Los Angeles, CA 90048

Michael Beach
10100 Santa Monica Blvd., #2500
Los Angeles, CA 90067

Jennifer Beals
14755 Ventura Blvd. #710
Sherman Oaks, CA 91403

Allyce Beasley
147 N. Windsor Blvd.
Los Angeles, CA 90004

Ned Beatty
2706 N. Beachwood Drive
Los Angeles, CA 90028

Warren Beatty
13671 Mulholland Drive
Beverly Hills, CA 90210

Jason Beghe
7473 Mulholland Drive
Los Angeles, CA 90046

Shari Belafonte-Harper
3546 Longridge Avenue
Sherman Oaks, CA 91423

Kathleen Beller
11288 Ventura Blvd., #304
Studio City, CA 91604

Jean-Paul Belmondo
9 rue des Sts-Peres
F-75006 Paris FRANCE

James Belushi
8033 Sunset Blvd. #88
Los Angeles, CA 90046

Dirk Benedict
4605 Lankershim Blvd., #305
North Hollywood, CA 91601

Annette Bening
13671 Mulholland Drive
Beverly Hills, CA 90210

Richard Benjamin
719 N. Foothill Road
Beverly Hills, CA 90210

Daniel Benzali
9016 Wilshire Blvd., #363
Beverly Hills, CA 90211

Tom Berenger
P.O. Box 1842
Beaufort, SC 29901

Candice Bergen
955 S. Carrillo Drive #200
Los Angeles, CA 90048

Peter Bergman
4799 White Oak Avenue
Encino, CA 91316

Milton Berle
10490 Wilshire Blvd. #1603
Los Angeles, CA 90024

Corbin Bernsen
3541 North Knoll Drive
Los Angeles, CA 90068

Halle Berry
1122 S. Robertson Blvd #15
Los Angeles, CA 90035

Ken Berry
15831 Foothill Blvd.
Sylmar, CA 91342

Valerie Bertinelli
P.O. Box 1984
Studio City, CA 91614

Mayim Bialik
8942 Wilshire Blvd.
Beverly Hills, CA 90211

Michael Biehn
11220 Valley Spring Lane
No. Hollywood, CA 91602

Barbara Billingsley
P.O. Box 1588
Pacific Palisades, CA 90272

Traci Bingham
5433 Beethoven Street
Los Angeles, CA 90066

Thora Birch
9560 Wilshire Blvd., #500
Beverly Hills, CA 90212

David Birney
20 Ocean Park Blvd. #11
Santa Monica, CA 90405

Joey Bishop
534 Via Lido Nord
Newport Beach, CA 92660

Jacqueline Bisset
1815 Benedict Canyon Drive
Beverly Hills, CA 90210

Yannick Bisson
55A Sumuch Street
Toronto Ontario
M5A 3J6 CANADA

Honor Blackman
11 Southwick Mews
London W2 1JG ENGLAND

Linda Blair
8033 Sunset Blvd. #204
Los Angeles, CA 90046

Robert Blake
11604 Dilling Street
N. Hollywood, CA 91608

Susan Blakely
421 N. Rodeo Drive, #15-111
Beverly Hills, CA 90210

Tempestt Bledsoe
10100 Santa Monica Blvd., #3490
Los Angeles, CA 90067

Wolf Blitzer
8929 Holly Leaf Lane
Bethesda, MD 20817

Lindsay Bloom
P.O. Box 412
Weldon, CA 93263

Michael Boatman
1571 S. Kiowa Crest Drive
Diamond Bar, CA 91765

Heidi Bohay
48 Main Street
S. Bound Brook, NJ 08880

Lisa Bonet
1551 Will Geer Road
Topanga, CA 90290

David Boreanaz
400 South Beverly Drive #216
Beverly Hills, CA 90212

Ernest Borgnine
3055 Lake Glen Drive
Beverly Hills, CA 90210

Tom Bosley
2822 Royston Place
Beverly Hills, CA 90210

Barry Bostwick
1640 South Sepulveda Blvd., #218
Los Angeles, CA 90025

Bruce Boxleitner
23679 Calabasas Road #181
Calabasas, CA 91302

Lara Flynn Boyle
12190 1/2 Ventura Blvd., #304
Studio City, CA 91604

Ed Bradley
285 Central Park West
New York, NY 10024

Kenneth Branagh
Studios Road
Shepperton, Middlesex
TW17 0QD ENGLAND

Marlon Brando
13828 Weddington
Van Nuys, CA 91401

Eileen Brennan
974 Mission Terrace
Camarillo, CA 91310

David Brenner
1575 Silver King Drive
Aspen, CO 81611

Beau Bridges
5525 N. Jed Smith Road
Hidden Hills, CA 91302

Jeff Bridges
985 Hot Springs Road
Montecito, CA 93108

Wilford Brimley
415 N. Camden Drive, #121
Beverly Hills, CA 90210

Morgan Brittany
3434 Cornell Road
Agoura Hills, CA 91301

Matthew Broderick
P.O. Box 69646
Los Angeles, CA 90069

Tom Brokaw
941 Park Avenue #14C
New York, NY 10025

James Brolin
6838 Zumirez Drive
Malibu, CA 90265

Charles Bronson
P.O. Box 2644
Malibu, CA 90265

Jayne Brook
9150 Wilshire Blvd., #350
Beverly Hills, CA 90212

Albert Brooks
1880 Century Park E. #900
Los Angeles, CA 90067

Mel Brooks
2301 La Mesa Drive
Santa Monica, CA 90405

Pierce Brosnan
23715 W. Malibu Road
Malibu, CA 90265

Rebecca Broussard
9911 W. Pico Blvd., PH #A
Los Angeles, CA 90035

Georg Stanford Brown
2565 Greenvalley Road
Los Angeles, CA 90046

Ellen Burstyn
P.O. Box 217
Palisades, NY 10964

Roscoe Lee Browne
3531 Wonderview Drive
Los Angeles, CA 90068

Gary Busey
18424 Coastline Drive
Malibu, CA 90265

Genevieve Bujold
27258 Pacific Coast Hwy.
Malibu, CA 90265

Jake Busey
18424 Coastline Drive
Malibu, CA 90265

Sandra Bullock
291 S. La Cienega Blvd. #616
Beverly Hills, CA 90211

Timothy Busfield
39-100 Z-Line Road
Clarksburg, CA 95613

Richard Burgi
2622 Victoria Blvd.
Laguna Beach, CA 92651

Brett Butler
4370 Tujunga Avenue #150
Studio City, CA 91604

Carol Burnett
7800 Beverly Blvd.
Los Angeles, CA 90036

Yancy Butler
6154 Glen Tower
Los Angeles, CA 90068

C   C

James Caan
P.O. Box 6646
Denver, CO 80206

Nicholas Cage
363 Copa de Oro
Los Angeles, CA 90077

Sid Caesar
1910 Loma Vista Drive
Beverly Hills, CA 90210

Dean Cain
11718 Barrington Court #513
Los Angeles, CA 90049

Stephen Caffrey
12338 Cantura Street
Studio City, CA 91604

Michael Caine
Rectory Farm House
North Stoke
Oxfordshire ENGLAND

Kirk Cameron
P.O. Box 8665
Calabasas, CA 91372

Colleen Camp
473 North Tigertail Road
Los Angeles, CA 90049

Bill Campbell
8942 Wilshire Blvd.
Beverly Hills, CA 90211

Neve Campbell
101-1184 Denman Street, Box 119
Vancouver BC V7G 2M9 CANADA

Tisha Campbell
5750 Wilshire Blvd., #640
Los Angeles, CA 90036

Dyan Cannon
8033 Sunset Blvd. #254
Los Angeles, CA 90046

Kate Capshaw
P.O. Box 869
Pacific Palisades, CA 90272

George Carlin
11911 San Vicente Blvd., #348
Los Angeles, CA 90049

Art Carney
RR 20, Box 911
Westbrook, CT 06498

David Carradine
628 South San Fermando Blvd., #C
Burbank, CA 91502

Keith Carradine
P.O. Box 460
Placerville, CO 81430

Robert Carradine
355 S. Grand Avenue #4150
Los Angeles, CA 90071

Tia Carrer
8228 Sunset Blvd. #300
Los Angeles, CA 90046

Jim Carrey
P.O.Box 57593
Sherman Oaks, CA 91403

Diahann Carroll
9255 Doheny Road
Los Angeles, CA 90069

Johnny Carson
6962 Wildlife Road
Malibu, CA 90265

Dixie Carter
10635 Santa Monica Blvd. #130
Los Angeles, CA 90025

Helena Bonham Carter
7 W Heath Avenue
London NW11 7S ENGLAND

Lynda Carter
9200 Harrington Drive
Potomac, MD 20854

Nell Carter
8484 Wilshire Blvd. #500
Beverly Hills, CA 90211

Gabrielle Carteris
1925 Century Park East #2320
Los Angeles, CA 90067

Angela Cartwright
10143 Riverside Drive
Toluca Lake, CA 91602

Veronica Cartwright
12754 Sarah Street
Studio City, CA 91604

David Caruso
270 N. Canon Drive #1058
Beverly Hills, CA 90210

Joanna Cassidy
133 North Irving Blvd.
Los Angeles, CA 90004

Patrick Cassidy
10433 Wilshire Blvd. #605
Los Angeles, CA 90024

Gabrielle Cateris
12953 Greenleaf Street
Studio City, CA 91604

Phoebe Cates
1636-3rd. Avenue #309
New York, NY 10128

Maxwell Caufield
340 East 64th Street #25
New York, NY 10021

Dick Cavett
109 E. 79th Street, #2C
New York, NY 10021

Christopher Cazenove
9300 Wilshire Blvd., #555
Beverly Hills, CA 90212

George Chakiris
7266 Clinton Street
Los Angeles, CA 90036

Richard Chamberlain
3711 Round Top Drive
Honolulu, HI 96822

Marilyn Chambers
3230 East Flamingo Road #202
Las Vegas, NV 89121

Marge Champion
484 West 43rd Street
New York, NY 10036

Jacki Chan
145 Waterloo Road
Kowloon HONG KONG, REPUBLIC OF
CHINA

Kyle Chandler
606 North Larchmont Blvd #309
Los Angeles, CA 90004

Carol Channing
9301 Flicker Way
Los Angeles, CA 90069

Stockard Channing
2801 Hutton Drive
Beverly Hills, CA 90210

Rosalind Chao
10100 Santa Monica Blvd. #2500
Los Angeles, CA 90067

Cyd Charisse
10724 Wilshire Blvd. #1406
Los Angeles, CA 90024

Chevy Chase
955 South Carrillo Drive #200
Los Angeles, CA 90048

Don Cheadle
2454 Glyndon Avenue
Venice, CA 90291

Anna Chlumsky
70 West Hubbard #200
Chicago, IL 60610

Rae Dawn Chong
4526 Wilshire Blvd.
Los Angeles, CA 90010

Julie Christie
23 Linden Gardens
London, W2 4HD, ENGLAND

William Christopher
P.O. Box 50698
Pasadena, CA 91105

Connie Chung
1 West 72nd Street
New York, NY 10023

Thomas Haden Church
8969 Sunset Blvd.
Los Angeles, CA 90069

Andrew (Dice) Clay
836 N. La Cienega Blvd., #202
Los Angeles, CA 90069

Jill Clayburgh
P.O. Box 18
Lakeville, CT 06039

John Cleese
82 Ladbroke Road
London, W11 3NU, ENGLAND

Glenn Close
9830 Wilshire Blvd
Beverly HIlls, CA 90212

James Coburn
1607 Schuyler Road
Beverly Hills, CA 90210

Michael Cole
6332 Costello Avenue
Van Nuys, CA 91401

Dabney Coleman
360 N. Kenter Avenue
Los Angeles, CA 90049

Gary Coleman
4710 Don Miguel Drive
Los Angeles, CA 90008

Lisa Coleman
3105 Ledgewood
Los Angeles, CA 90068

Gary Collins
2751 Hutton Place
Beverly Hills, CA 90210

Joan Collins
9255 Doheny Road
Los Angeles, CA 90069

Jeffrey Combs
13601 Ventura Blvd. #349
Sherman Oaks, CA 91423

Jeff Conaway
3162 Durand Drive
Los Angeles, CA 90068

Sean Connery
9830 Wilshire Blvd.
Beverly Hills, CA 90212

Carol Connors
1709 Ferrari Drive
Beverly Hills, CA 90210

Mike Connors
4810 Louise Avenue
Encino, CA 91316

Robert Conrad
11300 W. Olympic Blvd. #610
Los Angeles, CA 90064

Shane Conrad
1999 Avenue of the Starts #2850
Los Angeles, CA 90067

Michael Constantine
513 W. 54th Street
New York, NY 10019

Gary Conway
11240 Chimney Rock Road
Paso Robles, CA 93446

Kevin Conway
1999 Avenue of the Stars #2850
Los Angeles, CA 90067

Tim Conway
P.O. Box 17047
Encino, CA 91416

Jackie Cooper
9621 Royalton
Beverly Hills, CA 90210

Teri Copley
5003 Coldwater Canyon Avenue
Sherman Oaks, CA 91423

Ellen Corby
9026 Harratt Street
Los Angeles, CA 90069

Bud Cort
955 S. Carrillo Drive, #300
Los Angeles, CA 90048

Bill Cosby
P.O. Box 4049
Santa Monica, CA 90411

Kevin Costner
P.O. Box 275
Montrose, CA 91021

Katie Couric
1100 Park Avenue #15A
New York, NY 10025

Peter Coyote
774 Marin Drive
Mill Valley, CA 94941

Yvonne Craig
P.O. Box 827
Pacific Palisades, CA 90272

Richard Crenna
16030 Ventura Blvd., #380
Sherman Oaks, CA 91423

Mark Curry
12115 Magnolia Blvd., #134
North Hollywood, CA 91607

Hume Cronyn
63-23 Carlton Street
Rego Park, NY 11374

Tim Curry
9560 Wilshire Blvd. #516
Beverly Hills, CA 90212

Cathy Lee Crosby
1223 Wilshire Blvd. #404
Santa Monica, CA 90403

Jane Curtin
10450 Revuelta Way
Los Angeles, CA 90077

Tom Cruise
14775 Ventura Blvd. #1-710
Sherman Oaks, CA 91403

Valerie Curtin
15622 Meadowgate Road
Encino, CA 91316

Billy Crystal
9830 Wilshire Blvd.
Beverly Hills, CA 90212

Jamie Lee Curtis
9830 Wilshire Blvd.
Beverly Hills, CA 90212

Macaulay Culkin
124 West 60th Street
New York, NY 10023

Tony Curtis
11831 Folkstone Lane
Los Angeles, CA 90077

Robert Culp
1270 Sunset Plaza Drive
Los Angeles, CA 90069

Lise Cutter
4526 Wilshire Blvd.
Beverly Hills, CA 90010

D _____ D

Maryam D'Abo
8391 Beverly Blvd. #200
Los Angeles, CA 90048

Willem Dafoe
33 Wooster Street #200
New York, NY 10013

Olivia d'Abo
1122 S. Robertson Blvd. #15
Los Angeles, CA 90035

Timothy Dalton
21 Golden Square #315
London, W1R 3PA, ENGLAND

Tyne Daly
515 Ocean Avenue #601
Santa Monica, CA 90402

Beverly D'Angelo
8033 Sunset Blvd. #247
Los Angeles, CA 90046

Patti D'Arbanville
125 Main Avenue
Sea Cliff, NY 11579

Rodney Dangerfield
530 East 76th Street
New York, NY 10021

Jeff Daniels
137 Park Street
Chelsea, MI 48118

Ted Danson
165 Copper Cliff Lane
Sedona, AZ 86336

Tony Danza
10202 W. Washington Blvd. #DLEANBL
Culver City, CA 90232

Jennifer Darling
P.O. Box 57593
Sherman Oaks, CA 91403

Robert Davi
1907 Vallecito Drive
San Pedro, CA 90732

Clifton Davis
141 Janine Drive
La Habra Heights, CA 90631

Ossie Davis & Ruby Dee
44 Cortland Avenue
New Rochelle, NY 10801

Pam Dawber
2236-A Encinitas Blvd.
Encinitas, CA 92024

Doris Day
P.O. Box 223163
Carmel, CA 93922

Sandra Dee
880 Hilldale Avenue #15
Los Angeles, CA 90069

Ellen DeGeneres
1122 South Roxbury Drive
Los Angeles, CA 90035

Olivia DeHavilland
Boite Postale 156-16
Paris Cedar 16-75764 FRANCE

Dana Delany
3435 Ocean Park Blvd., #201-N
Santa Monica, CA 90405

Michael DeLorenzo
8271 Melrose Avenue, #110
Los Angeles, CA 90046

Rebecca DeMornay
760 N. La Cienega Blvd. #200
Los Angeles, CA 90069

Patrick Dempsey
2644 N. Beachwood Drive
Los Angeles, CA 90068

Catherine Deneuve
76 Rue Bonaparte
F-75006 Paris FRANCE

Lydie Denier
5350 Sepulveda Blvd. #9
Sherman Oaks, CA 91411

Robert DeNiro
375 Greenwich Street
New York, NY 10013

Brian Dennehy
121 N. San Vicente Blvd.
Beverly Hills, CA 90211

Bob Denver
P.O. Box 269
Princeton, W. VA 24740

Johnny Depp
500 Sepulveda Blvd. #500
Los Angeles, CA 90049

Bo Derek
3625 Roblar
Santa Ynez, CA 93460

Bruce Dern
23430 Malibu Colony Road
Malibu, CA 90265

Laura Dern
2401 Main Street
Santa Monica, CA 90405

Loretta Devine
5816 Ernest Avenue
Los Angeles, CA 90034

Danny DeVito
P.O. Box 491246
Los Angeles, CA 90049

Joyce DeWitt
1250-6th Street #403
Santa Monica, CA 90401

Susan Dey
10390 Santa Monica Blvd. #300
Los Angeles, CA 90025

Leonardo DiCaprio
4325 Edenhurst Avenue
Los Angeles, CA 90039

Angie Dickinson
1715 Carla Ridge Drive
Beverly Hills, CA 90210

Phyliss Diller
163 S. Rockingham Road
Los Angeles, CA 90049

Matt Dillon
40 West 57th Street
New York, NY 10019

Donna Dixon
8955 Norma Place
Los Angeles, CA 90069

Kevin Dobson
3511 Sea Ledge Lane
Santa Barbara, CA 93109

Peter Dobson
1351 N. Crescent Heights #318
Los Angeles, CA 90046

Shannen Doherty
133 South Rodeo Drive #300
Beverly Hills, CA 90212

Elinor Donahue
4525 Lemp Avenue
N. Hollywood, CA 91602

Phil Donahue
420 E. 54th Street #22F
New York, NY 10022

Troy Donahue
1022 Euclid Avenue #1
Santa Monica, CA 90403

Sam Donaldson
1125 Crest Lane
McLean, VA 22101

James Doohan
P.O. Box 2800
Redmond, WA 98073

Stephen Dorff
9701 Wilshire Blvd., 10th Floor
Beverly Hills, CA 90212

Kirk Douglas
805 N. Rexford Drive
Beverly Hills, CA 90210

Michael Douglas
151 Central Park West
New York, NY 10023

Mike Douglas
1876 Chartley Road
Gates Mill, OH 44040

Leslie-Ann Down
6252 Paseo Canyon
Malibu, CA 90265

Robert Downey, Jr.
1350 1/2 North Harper Avenue
Los Angeles, CA 90046

Hugh Downs
157 Columbus Avenue
New York, NY 10023

Richard Dreyfuss
14820 Valley Vista Blvd.
Sherman Oaks, CA 91403

James Drury
P.O. Box 899
Cyprus, TX 77429

Julia Duffy
9255 Sunset Blvd. #1010
Los Angeles, CA 90069

Patrick Duffy
P.O. Box "D"
Tarzana, CA 91356

Olympia Dukakis
222 Upper Mountain Road
Montclair, NJ 07043

Patty Duke
5110 E. Dodd Road
Hayden, ID 83835

David Dukes
255 S. Lorraine Blvd.
Los Angeles, CA 90004

Faye Dunaway
P.O. Box 15778
Beverly Hills, CA 90209

Charles Durning
10590 Wilshire Blvd. #506
Los Angeles, CA 90024

Marj Dusay
1964 Westwood Blvd., #400
Los Angeles, CA 90025

Charles Dutton
1201 Alta Loma Road
Los Angeles, CA 90069

Robert Duvall
P.O. Box 520
The Plains, VA 22171

Shelly Duvall
Route 1, Box 377-A
Blanco, TX 78606

E   E

Alison Eastwood
62bd. de Sepastopol
F-75003 Paris FRANCE

Clint Eastwood
4000 Warner Blvd., #16
Burbank, CA 91522

Buddy Ebsen
P.O. Box 2069
Palos Verdes Peninsula, CA 90274

Barbara Eden
P.O. Box 5556
Sherman Oaks, CA 91403

Richard Edlund
13335 Maxella Avenue
Marina del Rey, CA 90292

Anthony Edwards
15260 Ventura Blvd. #1420
Sherman Oaks, CA 91403

Samantha Eggar
12304 Santa Monica Blvd. #104
Los Angeles, CA 90025

Nicole Eggert
20591 Queens Park
Huntington Beach, CA 92646

Jill Eikenberry
197 Oakdale Avenue
Mill Valley, CA 94941

Erika Eleniak
1640 South Sepulveda Blvd., #218
Los Angeles, CA 90025

Gordon Elliott
555 West 57th Street
New York, NY 10019

Sam Elliott
33050 Pacific Coast Hwy.
Malibu, CA 90265

Robert Englund
1616 Santa Cruz Street
Laguna Beach, CA 93651

Bill Engvall
8380 Melrose Avenue #310
Los Angeles, CA 90069

Emilio Estevez
P.O. Box 4041
Malibu, CA 90264

Erik Estrada
3768 Eureka Drive
Studio City, CA 91604

Linda Evans
6714 Villa Madera Drive S.W.
Tacoma, WA 98499

Greg Evigan
10433 Wilshire Blvd. #210
Los Angeles, CA 90024

F _____ **F**

Shelley Fabares
P.O. Box 6010 MSC 826
Sherman Oaks, CA 91413

Jeff Fahey
8942 Wilshire Blvd.
Beverly Hills, CA 90211

Bruce Fairbairn
9744 Wilshire Blvd. #308
Beverly Hills, CA 90212

Morgan Fairchild
2424 Bowmont Drive
Beverly Hills, CA 90210

Peter Falk
100 Universal City Plaza #507 1-B
Universal City, CA 91608

Deborah Farentino
9460 Wilshire Blvd. #700
Beverly Hills, CA 90210

Linda Farentino
10683 Santa Monica Blvd.
Los Angeles, CA 90025

Dennis Farina
955 South Carrillo Drive #300
Los Angeles, CA 90048

Shannon Farnon
12743 Milbank Street
Studio City, CA 91604

Richard Farnsworth
P.O. Box 215
Lincoln, NM 88338

Jamie Farr
53 Ranchero
Bell Canyon, CA 91307

Mike Farrell
MSC 826, Box 6010
Sherman Oaks, CA 91413

Shea Farrell
1930 Century Park W. #403
Los Angeles, CA 90067

Terry Farrell
9229 Sunset Blvd., #71D
Los Angeles, CA 90069

Mia Farrow
124 Henry Sanford Road
Bridgewater, CT 06752

Farrah Fawcett
3130 Antelo Road
Los Angeles, CA 90077

Alice Faye
P.O. Box 1356
Rancho Mirage, CA 92270

Alan Feinstein
9229 Sunset Blvd. #311
Los Angeles, CA 90069

Corey Feldman
3209 Tareco Drive
Los Angeles, CA 90068

Barbara Feldon
14 East 74th Street
New York, NY 10021

Norman Fell
4240 Promenade Way #232
Marina del Rey, CA 90292

Edith Fellows
2016 1/2 N. Vista Del Mar
Los Angeles, CA 90068

Conchata Ferrell
1347 N. Sewart Street
Los Angeles, CA 90028

Lou Ferrigno
P.O. Box 1671
Santa Monica, CA 90402

Chelsea Field
P.O. Box 5617
Beverly Hills, CA 90210

Sally Field
P.O. Box 492417
Los Angeles, CA 90049

Kim Fields
9034 Sunset Blvd., #250
Los Angeles, CA 90069

Ralph Fiennes
17 Broad Circle #12
London WC2B 5QN ENGLAND

Fyvush Finkle
8730 Sunset Blvd. #480
Los Angeles, CA 90069

Linda Fiorentino
9830 Wilshire Blvd.
Beverly Hills, CA 90212

Laurence Fishburne
4116 West Magnolia Blvd., #101
Burbank, CA 91505

Carrie Fisher
1700 Coldwater Canyon
Beverly Hills, CA 90210

Frances Fisher
8730 Sunset Blvd., #490
Los Angeles, CA 90069

Joely Fisher
9465 Wilshire Blvd., #430
Beverly Hills, CA 90212

Fionnula Flanagan
121 North San Vicente Blvd.
Beverly Hills, CA 90211

Susan Flannery
789 Riven Rock Road
Santa Barbara, CA 93108

Rhonda Fleming
10281 Century Woods Drive
Los Angeles, CA 90067

Louise Fletcher
1520 Camden Avenue #105
Los Angeles, CA 90025

Calista Flockhart
405 South Beverly Drive #500
Beverly Hills, CA 90212

Nina Foch
P.O. Box 1884
Beverly Hills, CA 90213

Megan Follows
121 N. San Vicente Blvd.
Beverly Hills, CA 90211

Bridget Fonda
9560 Wilshire Blvd.#516
Beverly Hills, CA 90212

Jane Fonda
1050 Techwood Drive N.W.
Atlanta, GA 30318

Peter Fonda
RR #38, Box 2024
Livingston, MT 59047

Joan Fontaine
P.O. Box 222600
Carmel, CA 93922

Faith Ford
4232 Agnes Avenue
Studio City, CA 91604

Glenn Ford
911 Oxford Way
Beverly Hills, CA 90210

Harrison Ford
3555 N. Moose Road
Jackson, WY 83001

Maria Ford
10110 Empyrean Way #304
Los Angeles, CA 90067

Frederic Forrest
513 Wilshire Blvd., #347
Santa Monica, CA 90401

Brian Forster
16172 Flamstead Drive
Hacienda Heights, CA 91745

Robert Forster
1115 Pine Street
Santa Monica, CA 90405

John Forsythe
3849 Roblar Avenue
Santa Ynez, CA 93460

William Forsythe
16027 Ventura Blvd., #420
Encino, CA 91436

Fabian Forte
6671 Sunset Blvd., #1502
Los Angeles, CA 90028

Jodie Foster
10900 Wilshire Blvd., #511
Los Angeles, CA 90024

Meg Foster
10100 Santa Monica Blvd. #2500
Los Angeles, CA 90067

Michael J. Fox
7 Peabody Court
Teaneck, NJ 07666

Robert Foxworth
1230 Benedict Canyon Drive
Beverly Hills, CA 90210

Jonathan Frakes
9135 Hazen Drive
Beverly Hills, CA 90210

Tony Franciosa
567 Tigertail Road
Los Angeles, CA 90049

Anne Francis
P.O. Box 3282
Palm Desert, CA 92260

Genie Francis
9135 Hazen Drive
Beverly Hills, CA 90210

Joanna Frank
1274 Capri Drive
Pacific Palisades, CA 90272

Bonnie Franklin
10635 Santa Monica Blvd. #130
Los Angeles, CA 90025

Mary Frann
10100 Santa Monica Blvd. #2490
Los Angeles, CA 90067

Dennis Franz
11805 Bellagio Road
Los Angeles, CA 90049

Brendan Fraser
2118 Wilshire Blvd., #513
Santa Monica, CA 90403

Mona Freeman
608 N. Alpine Drive
Beverly Hills, CA 90210

Morgan Freeman
c/o William Morris
1325 Avenue of the Americas
New York, NY 10019

Phyllis Frelich
8485-E Melrose Place
Los Angeles, CA 90069

Susan French
110 E. 9th Street #C-1005
Los Angeles, CA 90079

Matt Frewer
6670 Wildlife Road
Malibu, CA 90265

Sir David Frost
130 West 57th Street
New York, NY 10019

Soleil Moon Frye
2713 N. Keystone
Burbank, CA 91504

Annette Funicello
16102 Sandy Lane
Encino, CA 91316

Edward Furlong
9830 Wilshire Blvd.
Beverly Hills, CA 90211

Stephen Furst
3900 Huntercrest Court
Moorpark, CA 93021

G   G

Princess Zsa Zsa Gabor
1001 Bel Air Road
Los Angeles, CA 90077

Courtney Gains
3300 Dabney Avenue
Altadena, CA 91001

Zack Galligan
9300 Wilshire Blvd., #555
Beverly Hills, CA 90212

Teresa Ganzel
9300 Wilshire Blvd. #410
Beverly Hills, CA 90212

Andy Garcia
4323 Forman Avenue
Toluca Lake, CA 91602

James Garner
33 Oakmont Drive
Los Angeles, CA 90049

Janeane Garofalo
9560 Wilshire Blvd., #500
Beverly Hills, CA 90212

Teri Garr
9150 Wilshire Blvd. #350
Beverly Hills, CA 90212

Rebecca Gayheart
853-7th Avenue #9A
New York, NY 10019

Cynthia Geary
21121 Foxtail
Mission Viejo, CA 92692

Sarah Michelle Gellar
11350 Ventura Blvd. #206
Studio City, CA 91604

Lynda Day George
10310 Riverside Drive #104
Toluca Lake, CA 91602

Susan George
520 Washington Blvd. #187
Marina del Rey, CA 90292

Richard Gere
9696 Culver Blvd. #203
Culver Cith, CA 90232

Gina Gershon
120 W. 45 th Street #3601
New York, NY 10036

Estelle Getty
10960 Wilshire Blvd. #2050
Los Angeles, CA 90024

Leeza Gibbons
1760 Courtney Avenue
Los Angeles, CA 90046

Marla Gibbs
3500 W. Manchester Blvd. #267
Inglewood, CA 90305

Charles Gibson
1965 Broadway #500
New York, NY 10023

Mel Gibson
4000 Warner Blvd. #P3-17
Burbank, CA 91522

Melissa Gilbert
P.O. Box 57593
Sherman Oaks, CA 91413

Sara Gilbert
16254 High Valley Drive
Encino, CA 91436

Erica Gimpel
10100 Santa Monica Blvd., #2500
Los Angeles, CA 90067

Paul Michael Glaser
317 Georgina Avenue
Santa Monica, CA 90402

Sharon Gless
P.O. Box 48005
Los Angeles, CA 90048

Danny Glover
41 Sutter Street #1648
San Francisco, CA 94104

Tracey Gold
4619 Goodland Avenue
Studio City, CA 91604

Whoopi Goldberg
5555 Melrose Avenue #114
Los Angeles, CA 90038

Jeff Goldblum
2401 Main Street
Santa Monica, CA 90405

Ricky Paul Goldin
9320 Wilshire Blvd. #300
Beverly Hills, CA 90212

Valeria Golino
8033 Sunset Blvd. #419
Los Angeles, CA 90046

Michael Goorjian
9000 Sunset Blvd., #1200
Los Angeles, CA 90069

Mark Paul Gosselaar
27512 Wellsley Way
Valencia , CA 91354

Louis Gossett, Jr.
8306 Wilshire Blvd. #438
Beverly Hills, CA 90211

Elliott Gould
21250 Califa #201
Woodland Hills, CA 91367

Kelsey Grammer
3266 Cornell Road
Agoura Hills, CA 91301

Hugh Grant
76 Oxford Street
London W1N OAX ENGLAND

Peter Graves
9777 Wilshire Blvd. #815
Beverly Hills, CA 90212

Erin Gray
10921 Alta View
Studio City, CA 91604

Linda Gray
P.O. Box 5064
Sherman Oaks, CA 91403

Kathryn Grayson
2009 La Mesa Drive
Santa Monica, CA 90402

Brian Austin Green
1122 South Robertson Blvd., #15
Los Angeles, CA 90035

Michele Greene
P.O. Box 29117
Los Angeles, CA 90029

Jennifer Grey
7920 Sunset Blvd., #400
Los Angeles, CA 90069

Richard Grieco
2934 1/2 N Beverly Glen Circle
Suite #252
Los Angeles, CA 90077

Andy Griffith
P.O. Box 1968
Manteo, NC 27954

Melanie Griffith
3110 Main Street #205
Santa Monica, CA 90405

Thomas Ian Griffith
5444 Agnes Avenue
N. Hollywood, CA 91607

Sam Groom
3708 Barham Blvd., #D-305
Los Angeles, CA 90068

Robert Guillaume
4709 Noeline Avenue
Encino, CA 91436

Bryant Gumbel
524 West 57th Street
New York, NY 10019

Janet Gunn
9229 Sunset Blvd. #710
Los Angeles, CA 90069

Steve Guttenberg
15237 Sunset Blvd. #48
Pacific Palisades, CA 90272

Jasmine Guy
21243 Ventura Blvd. #101
Woodland Hills, CA 91364

H   H

Shelly Hack
1208 Georgina
Santa Monica, CA 90402

Mark Hamill
P.O. Box 1051
Santa Monica, CA 90406

Gene Hackman
118 S. Beverly Drive #1201
Beverly Hills, CA 90212

George Hamilton
139 South Beverly Drive #330
Beverly Hills, CA 90212

Larry Hagman
9950 Sulpher Mountain Road
Ojai, CA 93023

Linda Hamilton
8955 Norman Place
W. Hollywood, CA 90069

Corey Haim
150 Carlton Street
Toronto, Ontario M5A 2K1 CANADA

Tom Hanks
P.O. Box 900
Beverly Hills, CA 90213

Khrystyne Haje
P.O. Box 8750
Universal City, CA 91608

Daryl Hannah
Columbia Plaza Bldg. #8-153
Burbank, CA 91505

Anthony Michael Hall
7301 Vista Del Mar #B-101
Playa del Rey, CA 90293

Kadeem Hardison
19743 Valleyview Drive
Topanga, CA 90290

Arsenio Hall
9560 Wilshire Blvd., #516
Beverly Hills, CA 90212

Dorian Harewood
810 Prospect Blvd.l
Pasadena, CA 91103

Veronica Hamel
129 North Woodburn
Los Angeles, CA 90049

Mariska Hargitay
9274 Warbler Way
Los Angeles, CA 90069

Mark Harmon
2236 Encinitas Blvd. #A
Encinitas, CA 92024

Tess Harper
8484 Wilshire Blvd. #500
Beverly Hills, CA 90211

Valerie Harper
15301 Ventura Blvd., #345
Sherman Oaks, CA 91403

Woody Harrelson
10780 Santa Monica Blvd., #280
Los Angeles, CA 90025

Mel Harris
6300 Wilshire Blvd. #2110
Los Angeles, CA 90048

Neil Patrick Harris
8942 Wilshire Blvd.
Beverly Hills, CA 90211

Richard Harris
17 Grove Hill Road
London, SE5 8DF, ENGLAND

Jenilee Harrison
9744 Wilshire Blvd., #203
Beverly Hills, CA 90212

Kathryn Harrold
9255 Sunset Blvd. #901
Los Angeles, CA 90069

Mary Hart
150 S. El Camino Drive #303
Beverly Hills, CA 90212

Melissa Joan Hart
10880 Wilshire Blvd., #1101
Los Angeles, CA 90024

Mariette Hartley
10110 Empyrean Way #304
Los Angeles, CA 90067

Lisa Hartman-Black
8489 West 3rd Street
Los Angeles, CA 90048

David Hasselhoff
5180 Louise Avenue
Encino, CA 91316

Teri Hatcher
10100 Santa Monica Blvd. #410
Los Angeles, CA 90067

Rutger Hauer
32 Sea Colony Drive
Santa Monica, CA 90405

Wings Hauser
9450 Chivers Avenue
Sun Valley, CA 91352

Ethan Hawke
1775 Broadway #701
New York, NY 10019

Goldie Hawn
1491 Capri
Pacific Palisades, CA 90272

Anne Heche
1122 South Roxbury Drive
Los Angeles, CA 90035

Jessica Hecht
9150 Wilshire Blvd., #175
Beverly Hills, CA 90212

Katherine Helmond
5570 Old Highway 395 North
Carson City, NV 89701

Mariel Hemingway
P.O. Box 2249
Ketchum, ID 83340

Sherman Hemsley
15043 Valley Heart Drive
Sherman Oaks, CA 91403

Marilu Henner
2101 Castillian
Los Angeles, CA 90068

Pamela Hensley
9526 Dalegrove Drive
Beverly Hills, CA 90210

Pee Wee Herman
P.O. Box 29373
Los Angeles, CA 90029

Howard Hesseman
7146 La Presa
Los Angeles, CA 90068

Charlton Heston
2859 Coldwater Canyon
Beverly Hills, CA 90210

Christopher Hewitt
1422 N. Sweetzer #110
Los Angeles, CA 90069

Dwayne Hickman
P.O. Box 3352
Santa Monica, CA 90403

Catherine Hicks
15422 Brownwood Place
Los Angeles, CA 90077

Gregory Hines
377 W. 11th Street, PH#4
New York, NY 10014

Judd Hirsch
888-7th Avenue #602
New York, NY 10107

Shere Hite
P.O. Box 1037
New York, NY 10028

Dustin Hoffman
1926 Broadway #305
New York, NY 10023

Paul Hogan
8446 1/2 Melrose Avenue
Los Angeles, CA 90069

Hal Holbrook
9100 Hazen Drive
Beverly Hills, CA 90210

Polly Holliday
888 - 7th Avenue #2500
New York, NY 10106

Lauren Holly
13601 Ventura Blvd. #99
Sherman Oaks, CA 91423

Katie Holmes
217 East Alameda Avenue #203
Burbank, CA 91502

Robert Hooks
145 N. Valley Street
Burbank, CA 91505

Bob Hope
10346 Moorpark
N. Hollywood, CA 91602

Sir Anthony Hopkins
7 High Park Road
Kew, Surrey,
Richmond, TW9 3BL, ENGLAND

Lee Horsley
15054 E. Dartmouth
Aurora, CO 80014

Arliss Howard
P.O. Box 9078
Van Nuys, CA 91409

Ken Howard
11718 Barrington Court #300
Los Angeles, CA 90049

Ron Howard
9830 Wilshire Blvd
Beverly Hills, CA 90210

Season Hubley
46 Wavecrest Avenue
Venice, CA 90291

Whip Hubley
9000 Sunset Blvd. #1200
Los Angeles, CA 90069

Finola Hughes
270 N. Canon Drive, #1064
Beverly Hills, CA 90210

Miko Hughes
924 Westwood Blvd. #900
Los Angeles, CA 90024

Renee Humphrey
346 East 63rd Street #4A
New York, NY 10021

Helen Hunt
9171 Wilshire Blvd. #406
Beverly Hills, CA 90210

Marsha Hunt
13131 Magnolia Blvd.
Sherman Oaks, CA 91423

Holly Hunter
19528 Ventura Blvd. #343
Tarzana, CA 91356

Tab Hunter
223 N. Guadalupe Street, #292
Santa Fe, NM 87501

William Hurt
151 El Camino Drive
Beverly Hills, CA 90212

Anjelica Huston
57 Windward Avenue
Venice, CA 90291

Will Hutchins
P.O. Box 371
Glen Head, NY 11545

Betty Hutton
Harrison Avenue
Newport, RI 02840

Lauren Hutton
382 Lafayette Street #6
New York, NY 10003

I   I

Jeremy Irons
200 Fulham Road
London, SW10 9PN, ENGLAND

Chris Isaak
1655-38th Avenue
San Fransisco, CA 94122

Michael Ironside
2145 Sunset Crest Drive
Studio City, CA 91604

Judith Ivey
15760 Ventura Blvd. #1730
Encino, CA 91436

Amy Irving
7920 Sunset Blvd. #400
Los Angeles, CA 90046

James Ivory
250 W. 57th Street #1913-A
New York, NY 10019

J   J

Anne Jackson
90 Riverside Drive
New York, NY 10024

Mary Ann Jackson
1242 Alessandro Drive
Newbury Park, CA 91320

Glenda Jackson
51 Harvey Road
London, SE3, ENGLAND

Melody Jackson
6269 Selma Avenue #15
Los Angeles, CA 90028

Joshua Jackson
8211 Melrose Avenue #200
Los Angeles, CA 90046

Paul Jackson, Jr.
40 West 57th Street
New York, NY 10019

Kate Jackson
P.O. Box 57593
Sherman Oaks, CA 91403

Samuel L. Jackson
5128 Encino Avenue
Encino, CA 91316

Sherry Jackson
4933 Encino Avenue
Encino, CA 91316

Stoney Jackson
1602 N. Fuller Avenue #102
Los Angeles, CA 90046

Victoria Jackson
14631 Balgowan Road #2-5
Hialeah, FL 33016

Lou Jacobi
c/o William Morris
325 Avenue of the Americas
New York, NY 10019

Lawrence-Hilton Jacobs
3804 Evan #2
Los Angeles, CA 90027

Billy Jacoby
P.O. Box 46324
Los Angeles, CA 90046

Henry Jaglom
609 E. Channel Road
Santa Monica, CA 90402

John James
P.O. Box #9
Cambridge, NY 12816

Conrad Janis
1434 N. Genesee Avenue
Los Angeles, CA 90069

Famke Janssen
345 North Maple Drive #397
Beverly Hills, CA 90210

Lois January
225 N. Crescent Drive #103
Beverly Hills, CA 90210

Claude Jarman, Jr.
16 Tamal Vista Lane
Kentifield CA 94904

Graham Jarvis
15351 Via de las Olas
Pacific Palisades, CA 90272

Sybil Jason
P.O. Box 40024
Studio City, CA 91604

Gloria Jean
20309 Leadwell
Canoga Park, CA 91303

Marianne Jean-Baptiste
83-93 Shepparton Road
London MI 3DF ENGLAND

Anne Jeffreys
121 S. Bentley Avenue
Los Angeles, CA 90049

Peter Jennings
47 West 66th Street
New York, NY 10023

Salome Jens
1716 Ridgedale Avenue
Los Angeles, CA 90026

Ann Jillian
151 El Camino Drive
Beverly Hills, CA 90212

Glynis Johns
121 N. San Vicente Blvd.
Beverly Hills, CA 90211

Anne-Marie Johnson
3500 W. Olive Avenue #1400
Burbank, CA 91505

Arte Johnson
2725 Bottlebrush Drive
Los Angeles, CA 90024

Don Johnson
P.O. Box 6909
Burbank, CA 91510

Kristen Johnson
8033 Sunset Blvd., #4020
Los Angeles, CA 90046

Laura Johnson
1917 Weepah Way
Los Angeles, CA 90046

Lynn-Holly Johnson
405 W. Riverside Drive #200
Burbank, CA 91506

Michelle Johnson
10100 Santa Monica Blvd., #2500
Los Angeles, CA 90067

Rafer Johnson
6071 Bristol Parkway #100
Culver City, CA 90230

Russell Johnson
P.O. Box 11198
Bainbridge Island, WA 98110

Angelina Jolie
13340 Galewood Drive
Sherman Oaks, CA 91423

Dean Jones
500 N. Buena Vista
Burbank, CA 91521

Dub Jones
223 Glendale
Rusten, LA 71270

Grace Jones
89 Fifth Avenue, 7th Floor
New York, NY 10003

James Earl Jones
P.O. Box 610
Pawling, NY 12564

Janet Jones
9100 Wilshire Blvd. #1000W
Beverly Hills, CA 90212

Jenny Jones
454 N. Columbus Drive
Chicago, IL 60611

Marcia Mae Jones
4541 Hazeltine Avenue #4
Sherman Oaks, CA 91423

Marilyn Jones
P.O. Box 69405
Los Angeles, CA 90069

Sam J. Jones
10000 Santa Monica Blvd. #305
Los Angeles, CA 90067

Shirley Jones
701 N. Oakhurst Drive
Beverly Hills, CA 90210

Tommy Lee Jones
P.O. Box 966
San Saba, TX 76877

James Carroll Jordan
8333 Lookout Mountain Avenue
Los Angeles, CA 90046

William Jordan
10806 Lindbrook Avenue #4
Los Angeles, CA 90024

Jackie Joseph
111 N. Valley
Burbank, CA 91505

Louis Jourdan
1139 Maybrook
Beverly Hills, CA 90210

Milla Jovovich
23 Watts Street #600
New York, NY 10013

Gordon Jump
3285 Minnesota Avenue
Costa Mesa, CA 92625

K   K

David Kagen
6457 Firmament Avenue
Van Nuys, CA 91406

Madeline Kahn
975 Park Avenue #9A
New York, NY 10028

Helena Kallianotes
12830 Mulholland Drive
Beverly Hills, CA 90210

Steven Kampmann
801 Alma Real
Pacific Palisades, CA 90272

Steve Kanaly
4663 Grand Avenue
Ojai, CA 93023

Carol Kane
8106 Santa Monica Blvd., #1426
Los Angeles, CA 90046

Gabriel Kaplan
9551 Hidden Valley Road
Beverly Hills, CA 90210

Marvin Kaplan
7600 Claybeck Avenue
Burbank, CA 91505

Mitzi Kapture
4705 Ruffin Road
San Diego, CA 92123

William Katt
23508 Canzonet Street
Woodland Hills, CA 91367

Julie Kavner
25154 Malibu Road #2
Malibu, CA 90265

Lainie Kazan
9903 Santa Monica Blvd. #283
Beverly Hills, CA 90212

James Keach
P.O. Box 548
Agoura, CA 91376

Stacy Keach, Jr.
27525 Winding Way
Malibu, CA 90265

Stacy Keach, Sr.
8749 Sunset Blvd.
Los Angeles, CA 90069

Jean Kean
28128 W. Pacific Coast Hwy.
Malibu, CA 90265

Staci Keanan
8730 Sunset Blvd. #220W
Los Angeles, CA 90069

Michael Kearns
1616 Garden Street
Glendale, CA 91201

Diane Keaton
1015 North Roxbury Drive
Beverly Hills, CA 90210

Michael Keaton
11901 Santa Monica Blvd. #547
Los Angeles, CA 90025

Don Keefer
4146 Allott Avenue
Sherman Oaks, CA 91423

Howard Keel
394 Red River Road
Palm Desert, CA 92211

Bob Keeshan
40 West 57th Street #1600
New York, NY 10019

David Keith
9595 Wilshire Blvd., #801
Beverly Hills, CA 90212

Penelope Keith
66 Berkeley House
Hay Hill
London, SW3, ENGLAND

Martha Keller
5 rue St. Dominique
75007 Paris, FRANCE

Sally Kellerman
7944 Woodrow Wilson Drive
Los Angeles, CA 90046

Sheila Kelley
10390 Santa Monica Blvd., #300
Los Angeles, CA 90025

Moira Kelly
P.O. Box 5617
Beverly Hills, CA 90210

Roz Kelly
5614 Lemp Avenue
N. Hollywood, CA 91601

George Kennedy
10100 Santa Monica Blvd., #2500
Los Angeles, CA 90067

Jayne Kennedy-Overton
224 Barbour Street
Playa del Rey, CA 90293

Mimi Kennedy
9000 Sunset Blvd. #1200
Los Angeles, CA 90069

Patsy Kensit
132 Loundoun Road
St. John's Woods
London NW8 ENGLAND

Ken Kercheval
P.O. Box 325
Goshen, KY 40026

Joanna Kerns
P.O. Box 49216
Los Angeles, CA 90049

Sandra Kerns
620 Resolano Drive
Pacific Palisades, CA 90272

Deborah Kerr
Los Monteros
E-29600 Marbella
Malaga, SPAIN

Brian Kerwin
304 West 81st Street #2
New York, NY 10024

Evelyn Keys
999 N. Doheny Drive #509
Los Angeles, CA 90069

Mark Keyloun
1320 North Laurel #18
West Hollywood, CA 90048

Margot Kidder
220 Pine Creek Road
Livingston, MT 59047

Nichole Kidman
333 N. Maple Drive, #135
Beverly Hills, CA 90210

Val Kilmer
P.O. Box 362
Tesuque, NM 87574

Lincoln Kilpatrick
1710 Garth Avenue
Los Angeles, CA 90035

Richard Kind
1345 N. Hayworth Avenue #112
Los Angeles, CA 90046

Roslyn Kind
8871 Burton Way #303
Los Angeles, CA 90048

Andrea King
1225 Sunset Plaza Drive #3
Los Angeles, CA 90069

Larry King
10801 Lockwood Drive, #230
Silver Springs, MD 20901

Perry King
3647 Wrightwood Drive
Studio City, CA 91604

Ben Kingsley
New Penworth, Stratford Upon Avon
Warwickshire, OV3 7QX, ENGLAND

Kathleen Kinmont
6651 Vineland Avenue
North Hollywood, CA 91606

Greg Kinnear
3000 W. Alameda Avenue, #2908
Burbank, CA 91523

Nastassja Kinski
1000 Bel Air Place
Los Angeles, CA 90077

Bruce Kirby
629 North Orlando Avenue #3
Los Angeles, CA 90048

Phyllis Kirk
321M S. Beverly Drive
Beverly Hills, CA 90212

Sally Kirkland
151 El Camino Drive
Beverly Hills, CA 90212

Terry Kiser
9911 W. Pico Blvd., #1060
Los Angeles, CA 90035

Tawny Kitaen
650 Town Center Drive #1000
Costa Mesa, CA 92626

Werner Klemperer
44 W. 62nd Street, 10th Floor
New York, NY 10023

Kevin Kline
1636-3rd Avenue #309
New York, NY 10128

Richard Kline
14322 Mulholland Drive
Los Angeles, CA 90077

Patrica Klous
18095 Karen Drive
Encino, CA 91316

Jack Klugman
22548 Pacific Coast Hwy.
Malibu, CA 90265

Michael E. Knight
10100 Santa Monica Blvd. #2500
Los Angeles, CA 90067

Shirley Knight
19528 Ventura Blvd., #559
Tarzana, CA 91356

Don Knotts
1854 S. Beverly Glen #402
Los Angeles, CA 90025

Jeff Kober
P.O. Box 16758
Beverly Hills, CA 90209

Walter Koenig
P.O. Box 4395
N. Hollywood, CA 91607

Ted Koppel
11810 Glenn Mill Road
Potomac, MD 20854

Maria Korda
304 N. Screenland Drive
Burbank, CA 91505

Harvey Korman
1136 Stradella Road
Los Angeles, CA 90077

Yaphet Kotto
10100 Santa Monica Blvd., #2490
Los Angeles, CA 90067

Martin Kove
19155 Rostia Street
Tarzana, CA 91356

Harley Jane Kozak
2329 Stanley Hills Drive
Los Angeles, CA 90046

Linda Kozlowski
9150 Wilshire Blvd., #205
Beverly Hills, CA 90212

Stepfanie Kramer
9300 Wilshire Blvd. #555
Beverly Hills, CA 90212

Brian Krause
10683 Santa Monica Blvd.
Los Angeles, CA 90025

Sylvia Kristal
8955 Norma Place
Los Angeles, CA 90069

Lisa Kudrow
1122 South Robertson Blvd., #15
Los Angeles, CA 90035

Kari Kupcinet
1730 N. Clark Street #3311
Chicago, IL 60614

Swoosie Kurtz
320 Central Park West
New York, NY 10025

L _____ L

Mathew Laborteaux
4555 Mariota Avenue
Toluca Lake, CA 91602

Patrick Laborteaux
1450 Belfast Drive
Los Angeles, CA 90069

Alana Ladd
1420 Moraga Drive
Los Angeles, CA 90049

Cheryl Ladd
P.O. Box 1329
Santa Ynez, CA 93460

Diane Ladd
P.O. Box 17111
Beverly Hills, CA 90209

Christine Lahti
1122 South Robertson Blvd., #15
Los Angeles, CA 90035

41

Ricki Lake
401 Fifth Avenue
New York, NY 10016

Hedy Lamarr
568 Orange Drive #47
Altamonte Springs, FL 32701

Lorenzo Lamas
3727 West Magnolia Blvd. #807
Burbank, CA 91505

Martin Landau
7455 Palo Vista Drive
Los Angeles, CA 90046

Audrey Landers
3112 Nicka Drive
Los Angeles, CA 90077

Steve Landesberg
355 North Genesee Avenue
Los Angeles, CA 90069

Nathan Lane
P.O. Box 1249
White River Junction, VT 05001

Hope Lange
803 Bramble
Los Angeles, CA 90049

Ted Lange
18653 Ventura Blvd., #131-B
Tarzana, CA 91356

Heather Langenkamp
9229 Sunset Blvd. #311
Los Angeles, CA 90069

Angela Lansbury
635 Bonhill Road
Los Angeles, CA 90049

John Larroquette
P.O. Box 6910
Malibu, CA 90264

Eva LaRue-Callahan
11661 San Vicente Blvd., #307
Los Angeles, CA 90049

John Laughlin
11815 Magnolia Blvd. #2
N. Hollywood, CA 91607

John Phillip Law
1339 Miller Drive
Los Angeles, CA 90069

Carol Lawrence
12337 Ridge Circle
Los Angeles, CA 90049

Martin Lawrence
9560 Wilshire Blvd., #516
Beverly Hills, CA 90212

Vicki Lawrence
6000 Lido Avenue
Long Beach, CA 90803

Robin Leach
1 Dag Hammarskjold Plaza, 21st Fl.
New York, NY 10017

Michael Learned
1600 N. Beverly Drive
Beverly Hills, CA 90210

Matt LeBlanc
11766 Wilshire Blvd., #1470
Los Angeles, CA 90025

Kelly LeBrock
4526 Wilshire Blvd.
Los Angeles, CA 90010

Christopher Lee
21 Golden Square, #200
London W1R 3PA ENGLAND

Hyapatia Lee
15127 Califa Street
Van Nuys, CA 91411

Peggy Lee
11404 Bellagio Road
Los Angeles, CA 90024

Janet Leigh
1625 Summitridge Drive
Beverly Hills, CA 90210

Jennifer Jason Leigh
2400 Whitman Place
Los Angeles, CA 90068

Chris Lemmon
80 Murray Drive
S. Glastonbury, CT 06073

Jack Lemmon
141 S. El Camino Drive #201
Beverly Hills, CA 90212

Jay Leno
P.O. Box 7885
Burbank, CA 91510

Rula Lenska
306 - 16 Eustin Road
London NW13 ENGLAND

Melissa Leo
853-7th Avenue #9A
New York, NY 10019

Tea Leoni
2300 West Victory Blvd.
Burbank, CA 91506

Jared Leto
405 South Beverly Drive #500
Beverly Hills, CA 90212

David Letterman
1697 Broadway
New York, NY 10019

Daniel Day Lewis
46 Albermarle Street
London W1X 4PP ENGLAND

Dawnn Lewis
P.O. Box 56718
Sherman Oaks, CA 91413

Jerry Lewis
3160 W. Sahara Avenue #816
Las Vegas, NV 89102

Richard Lewis
345 N. Maple Drive #300
Beverly Hills, CA 90210

Judith Light
1475 Sierra Vista Drive
Aspen, CO 81611

Art Linkletter
1100 Bel Air Road
Los Angeles, CA 90077

Laura Linney
8942 Wilshire Blvd.
Beverly Hills, CA 90211

Ray Liotta
16829 Monte Hermosa Drvie
Pacific Palisades, CA 90272

John Lithgow
1319 Warnall Avenue
Los Angeles, CA 90024

Dennis Lipscomb
9200 Sunset Blvd., #1113
Los Angeles, CA 90069

Stephen Liska
15050 Sherman Way #167
Van Nuys, CA 91405

Rich Little
5485 W. Flamingo Road #105
Las Vegas, NV 89103

Christopher Lloyd
P.O. Box 491246
Los Angeles, CA 90049

Kathleen Lloyd
116 Rosehedge Lane
Agoura, CA 91301

Norman Lloyd
1813 Old Ranch Road
Los Angeles, CA 90049

June Lockhart
P.O. Box 3207
Santa Monica, CA 90403

Heather Locklear
1836 Courtney Terrace
Los Angeles, CA 90046

Robert Loggia
544 Bellagio Terrace
Los Angeles, CA 90049

Julie London
16074 Royal Oaks
Encino, CA 91436

Shelly Long
15237 Sunset Blvd.
Pacific Palisades, CA 90272

Traci Lords
P.O. Box 16758
Beverly Hills, CA 90209

Sophia Loren
1151 Hidden Valley Road
Thousand Oaks, CA 91360

Lori Loughlin
1122 South Robertson Blvd., #15
Los Angeles, CA 90035

Tina Louise
310 E. 46th Street #18-T
New York, NY 10017

Linda Lovelace (Marciano)
120 Enterprise
Secaucus, NJ 07094

Jon Lovitz
4735 Viviana Drive
Tarzana, CA 91356

Dale Lowdermilk
P.O. Box 5743
Montecito, CA 93150

Chad Lowe
7920 Sunset Blvd., 4th Floor
Los Angeles, CA 90046

Rob Lowe
646 Romero Canyon Road
Santa Barbara, CA 93108

Susan Lucci
P.O. Box 621
Quogue, NY 11959

Lorna Luft
108 East Matilija Street
Ojai, CA 93023

Joan Lunden
1965 Broadway #400
New York, NY 10023

Kelly Lynch
1970 Mandeville Canyon Road
Los Angeles, CA 90049

M   M

Ali MacGraw
10345 W. Olympic Blvd. #200
Los Angeles, CA 90064

Stephen Macht
248 S. Rodeo Drive
Beverly Hills, CA 90212

Kyle MacLachlan
132 S. Rodeo Drive #300
Beverly Hills, CA 90212

Shirley MacLaine
25200 Old Malibu Road
Malibu, CA 90265

Patrick MacNee
P.O. Box 1685
Palm Springs, CA 92263

William H. Macy
405 South Beverly Drive #500
Beverly Hills, CA 90212

Michael Madsen
9830 Wilshire Blvd.
Beverly Hills, CA 90212

Virginia Madsen
9830 Wilshire Blvd.
Beverly Hills, CA 90212

Debra Maffett
1525 McGavock Street
Nashville, TN 37203

Bill Maher
7800 Beverly Blvd. #D
Los Angeles, CA 90036

Robert Maheu
3523 Cochise Lane
Las Vegas, NV 89109

Lee Majors
3000 Holiday Drive PH #1
Ft. Lauderdale, FL 33316

Chris Makepeace
P.O. Box 1095, Station Q
Toronto, Ont. M4T 2P2 CANADA

Kristina Malandro
P.O. Box 491035
Los Angeles, CA 90049

Karl Malden
1845 Mandeville Canyon Road
Los Angeles, CA 90049

Nick Mancuso
3500 W. Olive Avenue #1400
Burbank, CA 91505

Howie Mandell
8942 Wilshire Blvd.
Beverly Hills, CA 90211

Marla Maples
721 Fifth Avenue
New York, NY 10022

Sophie Marceau
13 rue Madeleine Michelle
F-92200 Neuilly-sur-Seine FRANCE

Ann-Margret (Smith)
151 El Camino Drive
Beverly Hills, CA 90212

Julianne Margulies
405 South Beverly Drive #500
Beverly Hills, CA 90212

E.G. Marshall
RFD #2, Orego Road
Mount Kisco, NY 10549

Penny Marshall
8942 Wilshire Blvd.
Beverly Hills, CA 90212

Peter Marshall
16714 Oakview Drive
Encino, CA 91316

Jared Martin
9300 Wilshire Blvd., #500
Beverly Hill, CA 90212

Pamela Sue Martin
1199 Forest Avenue #275
Pacific Grove, CA 93951

Steve Martin
P.O. Box 929
Beverly Hills, CA 90213

Wink Martindale
5744 Newcastle
Calabasas, CA 91302

A. Martinez
6835 Wild Life Road
Malibu, CA 90265

Marsha Mason
320 Galisted Street #305
Santa Fe, NM 87401

Tom Mason
853 - 7th Avenue #9A
New York, NY 10019

Mary Stuart Masterson
P.O. Box 1249
White River Junction, VT 05001

Jerry Mathers
31103 Rancho Viejo Road #2143
San Juan Capistrano, CA 92675

Tim Matheson
9171 Wilshire Blvd., #406
Beverly Hills, CA 90210

Marlee Matlin
7920 Sunset Blvd., #400
Los Angeles, CA 90046

Walter Matthau
278 Toyopa Drive
Pacific Palisades, CA 90272

Brad Maule
4136 Dixie Canyon
Sherman Oaks, CA 91423

Virginia Mayo
109 E. Avenue De Los Arboles
Thousand Oaks, CA 91360

David McCallum
68 Old Brompton Road
London SW7 3LQ ENGLAND

Andrew McCarthy
8942 Wilshire Blvd
Beverly Hills, CA 90211

Jenny McCarthy
345 North Maple Drive #185
Beverly Hills, CA 90210

Kevin McCarthy
14854 Sutton Street
Sherman Oaks, CA 91403

Nobu McCarthy
9229 Sunset Blvd., #311
Los Angeles, CA 90069

Mary McCormack
P.O. Box 67335
Los Angeles, CA 90067

Matt McCoy
4526 Wilshire Blvd.
Los Angeles, CA 90010

James McDaniel
8730 Sunset Blvd. #480
Los Angeles, CA 90069

Roddy McDowell
3110 Brookdale Road
Studio City, CA 91604

Darren McGavin
P.O. Box 2939
Beverly Hills, CA 90213

Vonetta McGee
1801 Avenue of the Stars, #902
Los Angeles, CA 90067

Kelly McGillis
303 Whitehead Street
Key West, FL 33040

Patrick McGoohan
16808 Bollinger Drive
Pacific Palisades, CA 90272

Elizabeth McGovern
17319 Magnolia Blvd.
Encino, CA 91316

Ewan McGregor
503/504 Lotts Road
The Chambers
Chelsea Harbour
SWIO OXF ENGLAND

Dorothy McGuire
10351 Santa Monica Blvd. #300
Los Angeles, CA 90025

Michael McKean
833 Thornhill Road
Calabasas, CA 91302

Nancy McKeon
P.O. Box 6778
Burbank, CA 91510

Philip McKeon
11409 Dona Dorotea Drive
Studio City, CA 91604

Rachel McLish
120 South El Camino Drive #116
Beverly Hills, CA 90212

Ed McMahon
12000 Crest Court
Beverly Hills, CA 90210

William McNamara
21154 Entrada Road
Topanga, CA 90290

Kristy McNichol
151 El Camino Drive
Beverly Hills, CA 90212

Chad McQueen
8306 Wilshire Blvd. #438
Beverly Hills, CA 90211

Jayne Meadows (Allen)
15201 Burbank Blvd.
Van Nuys, CA 91411

Lee Ann Meriwether
P.O. Box 260402
Encino, CA 91326

Laurie Metcalf
11845 Kling Street
N. Hollywood, CA 91607

Guy Michelmore
72 Goldsmith Avenue
London W3 6HN ENGLAND

Joanna Miles
2062 N. Vine Street
Los Angeles, CA 90068

Sarah Miles
Chithurst Manor
Trotton nr. Petersfield
Hampshire GU31 5EU ENGLAND

Dennis Miller
40 West 57th Street
New York, NY 10019

Johnny Lee Miller
870 Sunset Blvd. #490
Los Angeles, CA 90069

Penelope Ann Miller
P.O. Box 7369
Santa Monica, CA 90406

Donna Mills
2260 Benedict Canyon Drive
Beverly Hills, CA 90210

Hayley Mills
81 High Street
Hampton, Middlesex, ENGLAND

Yvette Mimieux
500 Perugia Way
Los Angeles, CA 90077

Kim Miyori
121 N. San Vicente Blvd.
Beverly Hills, CA 90211

Mary Ann Mobley
2751 Hutton Drive
Beverly Hills, CA 90210

Matthew Modine
9696 Culver Blvd. #203
Culver City, CA 90232

D.W. Moffett
450 N. Rossmore Avenue #401
Los Angeles, CA 90004

Jay Mohr
9200 Sunset Blvd., #1130
Los Angeles, CA 90069

Richard Moll
1119 N. Amalfi Drive
Pacific Palisades, CA 90272

Ricardo Montalban
1423 Oriole Drive
Los Angeles, CA 90069

Clayton Moore
4720 Parkolivo
Calabasas, CA 91302

Demi Moore
955 South Carrillo Drive #200
Los Angeles, CA 90048

Dudley Moore
73 Market Street
Venice, CA 90291

Julianne Moore
8912 Burton Way
Beverly Hills, CA 90211

Mary Tyler Moore
510 E. 86th Street, #21A
New York, NY 10028

Melba Moore
c/o HUSH
231 West 58th Street
New York, NY 10019

Roger Moore
2-4 Noel Street
London, W1V 3RB, ENGLAND

Esai Morales
1147 S. Wooster Street
Los Angeles, CA 90035

Rita Moreno
1620 Amalfi Drive
Pacific Palisades, CA 90272

Harry Morgan
13172 Boca De Canon Lane
Los Angeles, CA 90049

Jaye P. Morgan
1185 La Grange Avenue
Newbury park, CA 91320

Cathy Moriarty
1100 Alta Loma Road #801
West Hollywood, CA 90069

Michael Moriarty
200 W. 58th Street #3B
New York, NY 10019

Noriyuki "Pat" Morita
P.O. Box 491278
Los Angeles, CA 90049

Robert Morse
13830 Davana Terrace
Sherman Oaks, CA 91403

Kate Moss
5 Jubilee Place #100
London SW3 3TD ENGLAND

Bill Moyers
524 West 57th Street
New York, NY 10019

Armin Mueller-Stahl
c/o ZBF
Ordensmeisterstr. 15-16
D-12099 Berlin GERMANY

Patrick Muldoon
345 North Maple Drive #300
Beverly Hill, CA 90210

Chris Mulkey
918 Zenizia Avenue
Venice, CA 90291

Martin Mull
338 Chadbourne Avenue
Los Angeles, CA 90049

Greg Mullavey
P.O. Box 46067
West Hollywood, CA 90046

Richard Mulligan
1438 North Gower Street
Hollywood, CA 90028

Dermot Mulroney
5200 Linwood Drive
Los Angeles, CA 90027|

Billy Mumy
P.O. Box 856
North Hollywood, CA 91603

Ben Murphy
3601 Vista Pacifica #17
Malibu, CA 90265

Eddie Murphy
152 W. 57th Street #4700
New York, NY 10019

Bill Murray
P.O. Box 2267
Redondo Beach, CA 90278

Don Murray
1215-F De La Vina Street
Santa Barbara, CA 93101

N   N

Jim Nabor
P.O. Box 10364
Honolulu, HI 96816

Kathy Najimy
8383 Wilshire Blvd., #444
Beverly Hills, CA 90211

Hugo Napier
2207 N. Beachwood Drive
Los Angeles, CA 90068

Patricia Neal
45 E. End Avenue #4C
New York, NY 10028

Tracey Needham
9229 Sunset Blvd. #311
Los Angeles, CA 90069

Liam Neeson
200 Fulham Road
London SWIO 9PN ENGLAND

Craig T. Nelson
28872 Boniface Drive
Malibu, CA 90265

Judd Nelson
409 N. Camden Drive #202
Beverly Hills, CA 90210

Claudette Nevins
3500 W. Olive Avenue #1400
Burbank, CA 91505

Bob Newhart
420 Amapola Lane
Los Angeles, CA 90077

Paul Newman
1120-5th Avenue #IC
New York, NY 10128

Phyllis Newman
1501 Broadway #703
New York, NY 10036

Julie Newmar
204 Carmelina Avenue
Los Angeles, CA 90049

Nichelle Nichols
22647 Ventura Blvd.
Woodland Hills, CA 91364

Jack Nicholson
15760 Ventura Blvd. #1730
Encino, CA 91436

Julia Nickson
1206 South Hudson Avenue
Los Angeles, CA 90019

Brigitte Nielsen
P.O. Box 57593
Sherman Oaks, CA 91403

Leslie Nielsen
1622 Viewmont Drive
Los Angeles, CA 90069

Leonard Nimoy
2300 W. Victory Blvd., #C-384
Burbank, CA 91506

Nick Nolte
6174 Bonsall Drive
Malibu, CA 90265

Chuck Norris
P.O. Box 872
Navasota, TX 77868

Edward Norton
8000 Sunset Blvd. #300
Los Angeles, CA 90046

Deborah Norville
P.O. Box 426
Mill Neck, NY 11765

Michael Nouri
14 West 68th Street #12
New York, NY 10023

O   **O**

Hugh O'Brian
10880 Wilshire Blvd. #1500
Los Angeles, CA 90024

Conan O'Brien
30 Rockefeller Plaza
New York, NY 10012

Carrol O'Connor
30826 Broadbeach Road
Malibu, CA 90265

Donald O'Connor
P.O. Box 20204
Sedona, AZ 86341

Chris O'Donnell
P.O.Box 220250
St.Louis,MO 63112

Rosie O'Donnell
235 No. Broadway
Nyack, NY 10960

Maureen O'Hara
Box 1400, Christeansted
St. Croix, VI 00820

Miles O'Keeffe
1725-B Madison Avenue #625
Memphis, TN 38104

Soon-Tech Oh
128 North San Vicente Blvd.
Beverly Hills, CA 90211

Gary Oldman
76 Oxford Street
London W1N OAX ENGLAND

Ken Olin
5855 Topanga Canyon #410
Woodland Hills, CA 91367

Edward James Olmos
18034 Ventura Blvd. #228
Encino, CA 91316

Ryan O'Neal
21368 Pacific Coast Hwy.
Malibu, CA 90265

Jennifer O'Neil
1191 Cross Creek Road
Franklin, TN 37067

Michael Ontkean
P.O. Box 1212
Malibu, CA 90265

Haley Joel Osment
3000 West Alameda Avenue
Burbank, CA 91523

Bibi Osterwald
341 Carroll Park West
Long Beach, CA 90815

Annette O'Toole
360 Morton Street
Ashland, OR 97520

Peter O'Toole
31/32 Soho Square
London, W1V 5DG ENGLAND

Catherine Oxenberg
1526 N. Beverly Drive
Beverly Hills, CA 90210

P _____ **P**

Al Pacino
301 W. 57th Street #16-C
New York, NY 10019

Joanna Pacula
1465 Lindacrest Drive
Beverly Hills, CA 90210

Holly Palance
2753 Roscomare Avenue
Los Angeles, CA 90077

Jack Palance
785 Tucker Road #G-206
Tehachapi, CA 93561

Chazz Palminteri
375 Greenwich Street
New York, NY 10013

Bruce Paltrow
304-21st Street
Santa Monica, CA 90402

Gwyneth Paltrow
9830 Wilshire Blvd.
Beverly Hills, CA 90212

Anna Paquin
P.O. Box 9585
Wellington NEW ZEALAND

Eleanor Parker
2195 La Paz Way
Palm Spring, CA 92262

Fess Parker
P.O. Box 908
Los Olivos, CA 93441

Jamerson Parker
1604 N. Vista Avenue
Los Angeles, CA 90046

Sarah Jessica Parker
P.O. Box 69646
Los Angeles, CA 90069

Mandy Patinkin
200 West 90th Street
New York, NY 10024

Jason Patric
10683 Santa Monica Blvd.
Los Angeles, CA 90025

Adrian Paul
1154 South Point View Street
Los Angeles, CA 90035

Jane Pauley
271 Central Park W. #10E
New York, NY 10024

David Paymer
1506 Pacific Street
Santa Monica, CA 90405

Gregory Peck
P.O. Box 837
Beverly Hills, CA 90213

Thaao Penghlis
7187 Macapa Drive
Los Angeles, CA 90068

Chris Penn
9560 Wilshire Blvd. #516
Beverly Hills, CA 90212

Sean Penn
2049 Central Park E. #2500
Los Angeles, CA 90067

Joe Penny
10453 Sarah
N. Hollywood, CA 91602

Rosie Perez
10683 Santa Monica Blvd.
Los Angeles, CA 90025

Ron Perlman
P.O. Box 5617
Beverly Hills, CA 90210

Valerie Perrine
Via Toscana 1
I-00187 Rome ITALY

Luke Perry
8484 Wilshire Blvd. #745
Beverly Hills, CA 90211

Joe Pesci
P.O. Box 6
Lavallette, NJ 08735

Donna Pescow
9300 Wilshire Blvd. #555
Beverly Hills, CA 90212

Bernadette Peters
323 West 80th Street
New York, NY 10024

Michelle Pfeiffer
3727 West Magnolia Blvd., #300
Burbank, CA 91505

Regis Philbin
101 W. 67th Street #51A
New York, NY 10023

Julianne Phillips
1999 Avenue of the Starts #2850
Los Angeles, CA 90067

Lou Diamond Phillips
1122 South Robertson Blvd., #15
Los Angeles, CA 90035

Mitch Pileggi
9229 Sunset Blvd. #315
Los Angeles, CA 90069

Bronson Pinchot
9150 Wilshire Blvd. #350
Beverly Hills, CA 90212

Jada Pinkett
9560 Wilshire Blvd. #516
Beverly Hills, CA 90212

Brad Pitt
2705 Glendower
Los Angeles, CA 90027

Mary Kay Place
2739 Motor Avenue
Los Angeles, CA 90064

Suzanne Pleshette
P.O. Box 1492
Beverly Hills, CA 90213

Amanda Plummer
1925 Century Park E. #2320
Los Angeles, CA 90067

Christopher Plummer
49 Wampum Hill Road
Weston, CT 06883

Sidney Poitier
9255 Doheny Road
Los Angeles, CA 90069

Markie Post
10153 1/2 Riverside Drive #333
Toluca Lake, CA 91602

Annie Potts
P.O. Box 29400
Los Angeles, CA 90029

CCH Pounder
121 N. San Vicente Blvd.
Beverly Hills, CA 90211

Maury Povich
250 W. 57th Street #26W
New York, NY 10019

Jane Powell
150 W. End Avenue #26C
New York, NY 10023

Stefanie Powers
P.O. Box 5087
Sherman Oaks, CA 91403

Paula Prentiss
719 N. Foothill Road
Beverly Hills, CA 90210

Priscilla Presley
1167 Summit Drive
Beverly Hills, CA 90210

Jason Priestly
11766 Wilshire Blvd., #1610
Los Angeles, CA 90025

Richard Pryor
16847 Bosque Drive
Encino, CA 91436

Victoria Principal
120 S. Spalding Drive #205
Beverly Hills, CA 90212

Keshia Knight Pulliam
P.O. Box 866
Teaneck, NJ 07666

Andrew Prine
3364 Longridge Avenue
Sherman Oaks, CA 91403

Bill Pullman
8750 Holloway Drive
Los Angeles, CA 90069

Freddie Prinz, Jr
9830 Wilshire Blvd.
Beverly Hills, CA 90212

Linda Purl
10417 Ravenwood Court
Los Angeles, CA 90077

Q   Q

Dennis Quaid
9665 Wilshire Blvd., #200
Beverly Hills, CA 90212

Aiden Quinn
500 S. Buena Vista Ave. #206
Burbank, CA 91502

Randy Quaid
P.O. Box 17372
Beverly Hills, CA 90209

Anthony Quinn
P.O. Box 479
Bristol, RI 02809

Kathleen Quinlan
P.O. Box 861
Rockaway, OR 97136

Francesco Quinn
1230 N. Horn Avenue #730
Los Angeles, CA 90069

R   R

Steve Railback
11684 Ventura Blvd., #581
Studio City, CA 91604

Tony Randall
1 West 81st Street #6D
New York, NY 10024

Theresa Randle
1018 Meadowbrook Avenue
Los Angeles, CA 90019

Sally Jessy Raphael
510 W. 57th Street #200
New York, NY 10019

Phylicia Rashad
888-7th Avenue #602
New York, NY 10106

Dan Rather
524 West 57th Street
New York, NY 10019

Stephen Rea
861 Sutherland Avenue
London W9 ENGLAND

Peter Reckell
8033 Sunset Blvd. #4016
Los Angeles, CA 90046

Robert Redford
1101-E Montana Avenue
Santa Monica, CA 90403

Lynn Redgrave
21342 Colina Drive
Topanga, CA 90290

Vanessa Redgrave
21 Golden Square
London, W1R 3PA, ENGLAND

Christopher Reeve
RR #2
Bedford, NY 10506

Keanu Reeves
9460 Wilshire Blvd., #700
Beverly Hills, CA 90212

Duncan Regehr
2501 Main Street
Santa Monica, CA 90405

Tim Reid
11342 Dona Lisa Drive
Studio City, CA 91604

Judge Reinhold
626 Santa Monica Blvd. #113
Santa Monica, CA 90405

Paul Reiser
11845 W. Olympic Blvd. #1125
Los Angeles, CA 90064

Burt Reynolds
16133 Jupiter Farm Road
Jupiter, FL 33478

Debbie Reynolds
305 Convention Center Drive
Las Vegas, NV 89109

Ving Rhames
751-24th Street
Santa Monica, CA 90402

Alfonso Ribeiro
3353 Blair Drive
Los Angeles, CA 90068

Giovanni Ribisi
5750 Wilshire Blvd., #580
Los Angeles, CA 90036

Christina Ricci
8942 Wilshire Blvd.
Beverly Hills, CA 90211

Branscombe Richmond
5706 Calvin Avenue
Tarzana, CA 91356

Jason James Richter
10683 Santa Monica Blvd.
Los Angeles, CA 90025

Don Rickles
23750 Malibu Road
Malibu, CA 90265

Molly Ringwald
9454 Wilshire Blvd. #405
Beverly Hills, CA 90212

John Ritter
15030 Ventura Blvd. #806
Sherman Oaks, CA 91403

Geraldo Rivera
524 W. 57th Street #1100
New York, NY 10019

Joan Rivers
1 E. 62nd Street
New York, NY 10021

Jason Robards
200 West 57th Street #900
New York, NY 10019

Jane Robelot
524 West 57th Street
New York, NY 10019

Eric Roberts
132 S. Rodeo Drive #300
Beverly Hills, CA 90212

Julia Roberts
6220 Del Valle Drive
Los Angeles, CA 90048

Pernell Roberts
20395 Seaboard Road
Malibu, CA 90265

Tanya Roberts
2126 Ridgemont Drive
Los Angeles, CA 90046

Cliff Robertson
325 Dunemere Drive
La Jolla, CA 92037

Dale Robertson
P.O. Box 850707
Yukon, OK 73085

Holly Robinson
10683 Santa Monica Blvd.
Los Angeles, CA 90025

Debbie Rochon
P.O. Box 1299
New York, NY 10009

Lela Rochon
250 W. 57th Street #1610
New York, NY 10107

Mimi Rogers
11693 San Vicente Blvd. #241
Los Angeles, CA 90049

Mr. Rogers (Fred)
4802 - 5th Avenue
Pittsburgh, PA 15213

Tristan Rogers
8550 Holloway Drive #301
Los Angeles, CA 90069

Wayne Rogers
11828 La Grange Avenue
Los Angeles, CA 90025

Andy Rooney
254 Rowayton Avenue
Rowayton, CT 06853

Michael Rooker
P.O. Box 5617
Beverly Hills, CA 90210

Mickey Rooney
P.O. Box 5028
Westlake Village, CA 91362

Roseanne
5664 Cahuenga Blvd., #433
North Hollywood, CA 91601

Katharine Ross
33050 Pacific Coast Hwy.
Malibu, CA 90265

Isabella Rossellini
745 Fifth Avenue #814
New York, NY 10151

Richard Roundtree
8091 Selma Avenue
Los Angeles, CA 90046

Mickey Rourke
9150 Wilshire Blvd., #350
Beverly Hills, CA 90212

Misty Rowe
P.O. Box 11152
Greenwich, CT 06831

Gena Rowlands
7917 Woodrow Wilson Drive
Los Angeles, CA 90046

Zelda Rubinstein
8730 Sunset Blvd., #270
Los Angeles, CA 90069

Mercedes Ruehl
Box 178, Old Chelsea Station
New York, NY 10011

Jennifer Runyon
5130 North Lakemont Lane
Boise, ID 83703

Jane Russell
2934 Torito Road
Santa Barbara, CA 93108

Kurt Russell
1900 Avenue of the Stars #1240
Los Angeles, CA 90067

Meg Ryan
11718 Barrington Court #508
Los Angeles, CA 90049

Winona Ryder
350 Park Avenue #900
New York, NY 10022

S   S

Morely Safer
51 West 52nd Street
New York, NY 10019

Katey Sagal
7095 Hollywood Drive #792
Los Angeles, CA 90028

Bob Saget
9150 Wilshire Blvd., #350
Beverly Hills, CA 90212

Eva Marie Saint
10590 Wilshire Blvd. #408
Los Angeles, CA 90024

Pat Sajak
3400 Riverside Drive
Burbank, CA 91505

Soupy Sales
245 E. 35th Street
New York, NY 10016

Emma Samms
2934 1/2 N. Beverly Glen Circle
Suite #417
Los Angeles, CA 90077

Altana Sanchez-Gijon
8730 Sunset Blvd. #490
Los Angeles, CA 90069

Paul Sand
924 Westwood Blvd., #900
Los Angeles, CA 90024

Adam Sandler
5420 Worster Avenue
Van Nuys, CA 91401

Julian Sands
1287 Ozeta Terrace
Los Angeles, CA 90069

Chris Sarandon
9540 Hidden Valley Road
Beverly Hills, CA 90210

Susan Sarandon
40 West 57th Street
New York, NY 10019

Paul Satterfield
400 South Beverly Drive #101
Beverly Hills, CA 90212

Doug Savant
1015 E. Angeleno Avenue
Burbank, CA 91501

Diane Sawyer
77 West 66th Street
New York, NY 10023

Raphael Sbarge
8281 Melrose Avenue #200.
Los Angeles, CA 90046

Roy Scheider
P.O. Box 364
Sagaponack, NY 11962

Rick Schroder
9560 Wilshire Blvd. #500
Beverly Hills, CA 90212

Arnold Schwarzenegger
3110 Main Street #300
Santa Monica, CA 90405

Eric Schweig
P.O. Box 5163
Vancouver, B.C. V7B 1MB
CANADA

David Schwimmer
10390 Santa Monica Blvd., #300
Los Angeles, CA 90025

Annabella Sciorra
132 S. Rodeo Drive, #300
Beverly Hills, CA 90212

Tracy Scoggins
1131 Alta Loma Road #515
Los Angeles, CA 90069

George C. Scott
3211 Retreat Court
Malibu, CA 90265

Lizabeth Scott
8277 Hollywood Blvd.
Los Angeles, CA 90069

Willard Scott
30 Rockefeller Plaza #304
New York, NY 10012

Steven Seagal
4875 Louise
Encino, CA 91316

George Segal
515 North Robertson Blvd.
Los Angeles, CA 90048

Jerry Seinfeld
211 Central Park West
New York, NY 10024

Connie Selleca-Tish
9255 Sunset Blvd. #1010
Los Angeles, CA 90069

Tom Selleck
331 Sage Lane
Santa Monica, CA 90402

Jane Seymour
P.O. Box 548
Agoura, CA 91376

Ted Shackleford
12305 Valleyheart Drive
Studio City, CA 91604

Garry Shandling
9150 Wilshire Blvd., #350
Beverly Hills, CA 90212

Omar Sharif
18 rue Troyan
F-75017 Paris FRANCE

William Shatner
P.O. Box 7401725
Studio City, CA 91604

Helen Shaver
9171 Wilshire Blvd. #436
Beverly Hills, CA 90210

Ally Sheedy
132 South Rodeo Drive #300
Beverly Hills, CA 90212

Charlie Sheen
10580 Wilshire Blvd.
Los Angeles, CA 90024

Martin Sheen
6919 Dune Drive
Malibu, CA 90265

Cybill Shepherd
3930 Valley Meadow Road
Encino, CA 91436

Nicholette Sheridan
8730 Shoreham Drive #A
Los Angeles, CA 90069

Brooke Shields
2300 West Sahara #630
Las Vegas, NV 89192

Yoko Shimada
7245 Hillside Avenue #415
Los Angeles, CA 90046

Pauly Shore
8420 Cresthill Road #700
West Hollywood, CA 90069

Martin Short
760 N. La Cienega Blvd. #200
Los Angeles, CA 90069

Kathy Shower
8383 Wilshire Blvd. #954
Beverly Hills, CA 90211

Kin Shriner
3915 Benedict Canyon
Sherman Oaks, CA 91423

Wil Shriner
5313 Quakertown Avenue
Woodland Hills, CA 91364

Maria Shriver
3110 Main Street #300
Santa Monica, CA 90403

Elizabeth Shue
P.O. Box 464
South Orange, NJ 07079

Henry Silva
8747 Clifton Way #305
Beverly Hills, CA 90210

Ron Silver
955 South Carrillo Drive #300
Los Angeles, CA 90048

Alicia Silverstone
60 McCreery Drive
Hillsborough, CA 94010

Jean Simmons
636 Adelaide Place
Santa Monica, CA 90402

Sinbad
21704 Devonshire #13
Chatsworth, CA 91311

Marc Singer
11218 Canton Drive
Studio City, CA 91604

Tom Skerritt
9560 Wilshire Blvd., #516
Beverly Hills, CA 90212

Christian Slater
9150 Wilshire Blvd. #350
Beverly Hills, CA 90212

Allison Smith
1999 Avenue of the Stars #2850
Los Angeles, CA 90067

Buffalo Bob Smith
1005 Riverview Drive
Brielle, NJ 08730

Jaclyn Smith
10398 Sunset Blvd.
Los Angeles, CA 90077

Keely Smith
28011 Paquet Place
Malibu, CA 90265

Wil Smith
8436 West 3rd Street #650
Los Angeles, CA 90048

Jimmy Smits
Box 49922, Barrington Station
Los Angeles, CA 90049

Dick Smothers
6442 Coldwater Canyon Ave. #107-B
North Hollywood, CA 91606

Tom Smothers
6442 Coldwater Canyon Ave. #107-B
North Hollywood, CA 91606

Wesley Snipes
1888 Century Park E. #500
Los Angeles, CA 90067

Carrie Snodgress
16650 Schoenborn
Sepulveda, CA 91343

Tom Snyder
1225 Beverly Estates Drive
Beverly Hills, CA 90210

Suzanne Somers
8899 Beverly Blvd., #713
Los Angeles, CA 90048

Elke Sommer
Atzelaberger Street 46
D-19080 Maloffstein, GERMANY

Mira Sorvino
41 West 86th Street
New York, NY 10024

David Soul
4201 Hunt Club Lane
Westlake Village, CA 91361

Sissy Spacek
Beau Val Farm
Route 22, #640
Cobham, VA 22929

Kevin Spacey
120 W. 45th Street #3600
New York, NY 10036

David Spade
9150 Wilshire Blvd. #350
Beverly Hills, CA 90212

James Spader
9530 Heather Road
Beverly Hills, CA 90210

Jerry Springer
454 North Columbus Drive #200
Chicago, IL 60611

Robert Stack
321 St. Pierre Road
Los Angeles, CA 90077

Leslie Stahl
524 West 57th Street
New York, NY 10019

Frank Stallone
10668 Eastborne Avenue #206
Los Angeles, CA 90025

Sylvester Stallone
100 SE 32nd Road
Coconut Grove, FL 33129

John Stamos
9255 Sunset Blvd. #1010
Los Angeles, CA 90069

Florence Stanley
P.O. Box 48876
Los Angeles, CA 90048

Harry Dean Stanton
14527 Mulholland Drive
Los Angeles, CA 90077

Jean Stapleton
5757 Wilshire Blvd. #PH 5
Los Angeles, CA 90036

Mary Steenburgen
1201 Alta Loma
Los Angeles, CA 90069

Andrew Stevens
9300 Wilshire Blvd. #400
Beverly Hills, CA 90212

Stella Stevens
2180 Coldwater Canyon
Beverly Hills, CA 90210

Parker Stevenson
4526 Wilshire Blvd.
Los Angeles, CA 90010

Ben Stiller
9660 Wilshire Blvd. #516
Beverly Hills, CA 90212

Dean Stockwell
P.O. Box 6248
Malibu, CA 90264

Guy Stockwell
6652 Coldwater Canyon Avenue
North Hollywood, CA 91606

John Stockwell
344 S. Rossmore Avenue
Los Angeles, CA 90029

Madeleine Stowe
10345 W. Olympic Blvd. #200
Los Angeles, CA 90064

Marcia Strassman
302 North Almont Drive
Beverly Hills, CA 90211

Meryl Streep
9830 Wilshire Blvd.
Beverly Hills, CA 90212

Sally Struthers
9100 Wilshire Blvd., #1000 West
Beverly Hills, CA 90212

Donald Sutherland
760 N. La Cienega Blvd. #300
Los Angeles, CA 90069

Kiefer Sutherland
132 So. Rodeo Drive, #300
Beverly Hills, CA 90212

Bo Svenson
15332 Antioch Street #356
Pacific Palisades, CA 90272

Michael Swan
15315 Magnolia Blvd. #429
Sherman Oaks, CA 91403

Don Swayze
247 S. Beverly Drive #102
Beverly Hills, CA 90212

Patrick Swayze
132 So. Rodeo Drive, #300
Beverly Hills, CA 90212

D.B. Sweeney
25144 Malibu Road
Malibu, CA 90265

Loretta Swit
10100 Santa Monica Blvd. #2490
Los Angeles, CA 90067

T   T

Mr. T
15208 La Maida Street
Sherman Oaks, CA 91403

George Takei
419 North Larchmont Blvd., #41
Los Angeles, CA 90004

Elizabeth Taylor
P.O. Box 55995
Sherman Oaks, CA 91413

Leigh Taylor-Young
9229 Sunset Blvd. #710
Los Angeles, CA 90069

Meshach Taylor
10100 Santa Monica Blvd., 25th Flr.
Los Angeles, CA 90067

Noah Taylor
P.O. Box 5617
Beverly Hills, CA 90210

Jon Tenney
9560 Wilshire Blvd., #516
Beverly Hills, CA 90212

John Tesh
P.O. Box 6010
Sherman Oaks, CA 91413

Lauren Tewes
2739-31st Avenue South
Seattle, WA 98144

Alan Thicke
10505 Sarah
Toluca Lake, CA 91602

Tiffani-Amber Thiessen
3500 W. Olive Avenue #1400
Burbank, CA 91505

Roy Thinnes
17258 Madison Avenue #634
Memphis, TN 3810

Ernest Thomas
3350 Barham Blvd.
Los Angeles, CA 90068

Heather Thomas
1433 San Vicente Blvd.
Santa Monica, CA 90402

Marlo Thomas
420 E. 54th Street #22F
New York, NY 10022

Philip Michael Thomas
12615 West Dixie Hwy.
N. Miami, FL 33161

Richard Thomas
4963 Los Feliz Blvd.
Los Angeles, CA 90027

Brian Thompson
3500 West Olive Avenue #1400
Burbank, CA 91505

Emma Thompson
56 King's Road
Kingston-upon -Thames
KT2 5HF ENGLAND

Lea Thompson
P.O. Box 5617
Beverly Hills, CA 90210

Linda Thompson
3365 Cahuenga Blvd. West #450
Los Angeles, CA 90068

Gordon Thomson
3718 1/2 Multiview Drive
Los Angeles, CA 90068

Uma Thurman
9830 Wilshire Blvd.
Beverly Hills, CA 90212

Meg Tilly
321 S. Beverly Drive #M
Beverly Hills, CA 90212

Charlene Tilton
P.O. Box 1309
Studio City, CA 91614

Lily Tomlin
P.O. Box 27700
Los Angeles, CA 90027

Angel Tompkins
9612 Video Drive, #101
Los Angeles, CA 90035

Rip Torn
130 W. 42nd Street #2400
New York, NY 10036

Fred Travalena
4515 White Oak Place
Encino, CA 91316

Daniel J. Travanti
1077 Melody Road
Lake Forest, IL 60045

Nancy Travis
231 S. Cliffwood Avenue
Los Angeles, CA 90049

John Travolta
15821 Ventura Blvd., #460
Studio City, CA 91436

Alex Trebek
10202 W. Washington Blvd.
Culver City, CA 90232

Christy Turlington
344 E. 59th Street
New York, NY 10022

Kathleen Turner
163 Amsterdam Avenue #210
New York, NY 10023

Nicholas Turturro
5201 Calvin Avenue
Tarzana, CA 91356

Shannon Tweed
9300 Wilshire Blvd., #410
Beverly Hills, CA 90212

Cicely Tyson
315 West 70th Street
New York, NY 10023

U   U

Anneliese Uhlig
1519 Escalona Drive
Santa Cruz, CA 95060

Dr. Art Ulene
10810 Via Verona
Los Angeles, CA 90024

Liv Ullman
Hafrsfjordgst 7
0273 Oslo, NORWAY

Blair Underwood
4116 North Magnolia Blvd., #101
Burbank, CA 91505

Jay Underwood
9595 Wilshire Blvd., #505
Beverly Hills, CA 90212

Robert Urich
10061 Riverside Drive #1026
Toluca Lake, CA 91602

Bonnie Urseth
9255 Sunset Blvd., #515
Los Angeles, CA 90069

Peter Ustinov
11 Rue de Silly
92100, Boulogne, FRANCE

V _____ V

Karen Valentine
P.O. Box 1410
Washington Depot, CT 06793

Joan Van Ark
10950 Alta View Drive
Studio City, CA 91604

Jean-Claude Van Damme
10926 Owensmouth Avenue
Chatsworth, CA 91316

Mamie Van Doren
428 - 31st Street
Newport Beach, CA 92663

Dick Van Dyke
23215 Mariposa De Oro
Malibu, CA 90265

Jerry Van Dyke
1705 Jameson Street
Benton, AR 72015

Dick Van Patten
13920 Magnolia Blvd.
Sherman Oaks, CA 91423

Vincent Van Patten
13926 Magnolia Blvd.
Sherman Oaks, CA 91423

Robert Vaughn
88 Salem View Drive
Ridgefield, CT 06877

Abe Vigoda
8500 Melrose Avenue #208
W. Hollywood, CA 90069

Jan-Michael Vincent
151 El Camino Drive
Beverly Hill, CA 90212

Jon Voight
9660 Oak Pass Road
Beverly Hills, CA 90210

Max Von Sydow
avd C-G Rissbery, Box 5209
Stockholm, 10245 SWEDEN

Lark Voorhies
10635 Santa Monica Blvd., #130
Los Angeles, CA 90025

W _____ W

Lindsay Wagner
P.O. Box 188
Pacific Palisades, CA 90272

Robert Wagner
P.O. Box 933339
Los Angeles, CA 90093

Ken Wahl
480 Westlake Blvd.
Malibu, CA 90265

Jimmie Walker
332 Southdown Road
Lloyd Harbor, NY 11754

Mike Wallace
555 West 57th Street
New York, NY 10019

Barbara Walters
33 West 60th Street
New York, NY 10023

Jamie Walters
4702 Ethel Avenue
Sherman Oaks, CA 91423

Judge Joseph Wapner
16616 Park Lane Place
Los Angeles, CA 90049

Fred Ward
1214 Cabrillo Avenue
Venice, CA 90291

Megan Ward
1999 Avenue of the Stars #2850
Los Angeles, CA 90067

Sela Ward
289 S. Robertson Blvd. #469
Beverly Hills, CA 90211

Marsha Warfield
P.O. Box 691713
Los Angeles, CA 90069

Julie Warner
9830 Wilshire Blvd.
Beverly Hills, CA 90212

Malcolm-Jamal Warner
15303 Ventura Blvd. #1100
Sherman Oaks, CA 91403

Lesley Ann Warren
2934 Beverly Glen Circle #372
Los Angeles, CA 90077

Denzel Washington
4701 Sancola
Toluca Lake, CA 91602

Keenan Ivory Wayans
16405 Mulholland Drive
Los Angeles, CA 90049

Shawn Weatherly
12203 Octagon Street
Los Angeles, CA 90049

Carl Weathers
10960 Wilshire Blvd. #826
Los Angeles, CA 90024

Dennis Weaver
P.O. Box 257
Ridgeway, CO 81432

Sigourney Weaver
200 W. 57th Street #1306
New York, NY 10019

Bruce Weitz
5030 Arundel Drive
Woodland Hills, CA 91364

Raquel Welch
9903 Santa Monica Blvd., #514
Beverly Hills, CA 90212

Tahnee Welch
134 Duane Street #400
New York, NY 10013

George Wendt
23458 West Moon Shadows Drive
Malibu, CA 90265

Patricia Wettig
5855 Topanga Canyon #410
Woodland Hills, CA 91367

Wil Wheaton
2820 Honolulu #255
Verdugo City, CA 91043

Lisa Whelchel
30408 Olympic Street
Castaic, CA 91384

Forest Whitaker
1990 S. Bundy Drive #200
Los Angeles, CA 90025

Betty White
P.O. Box 491965
Los Angeles, CA 90049

Bradley White
8730 Sunset Blvd. #480
Los Angeles, CA 90069

Jaleel White
151 El Camino Drive
Beverly Hills, CA 90212

Vanna White
3400 Riverside Drive
Burbank, CA 91505

Stuart Whitman
749 San Ysidro Road
Santa Barbara, CA 93108

James Whitmore
4990 Puesta Del Sol
Malibu, CA 90265

Gene Wilder
1511 Sawtelle Blvd. #155
Los Angeles, CA 90025

Billy Dee Williams
18411 Hatteras Street #204
Tarzana, CA 91356

Cindy Williams
7023 Birdview Avenue
Malibu, CA 90265

Jobeth Williams
9911 W. Pico Blvd. #PH1
Los Angeles, CA 90035

Kimberly Williams
151 El Camino Drive
Beverly Hills, CA 90212

Montel Williams
435 W. 53rd Street
New York, NY 10019

Robin Williams
3145 Geary Blvd., #524
San Francisco, CA 94118

Bruce Willis
1122 South Robertson Blvd., #15
Los Angeles, CA 90035

Flip Wilson
21970 Pacific Coast Hwy.
Malibu, CA 90265

Mara Wilson
3500 West Olive, #1400
Burbank, CA 91505

Rita Wilson
P.O. Box 900
Beverly Hills, CA 90213

Paul Winfield
5693 Holly Oak Drive
Los Angeles, CA 90068

Oprah Winfrey
P.O. Box 909715
Chicago, IL 60690

Debra Winger
P.O. Box 9078
Van Nuys, CA 91409

Henry Winkler
P.O. Box 49914
Los Angeles, CA 90049

Kate Winslet
503/504 Lotts Road
The Chambers, Chelsea Harbour
London SWIO OXF, ENGLAND

Jonathan Winters
4310 Arcola Avenue
Toluca Lake, CA 91602

Shelly Winters
457 N. Oakhurst Drive
Beverly Hills, CA 90210

Billy Wirth
9255 Sunset Blvd., #1010
Los Angeles, CA 90069

Elijah Wood
9150 Wilshire Blvd., #350
Beverly HIlls, CA 90212

James Woods
760 N. La Cienega Blvd.
Los Angeles, CA 90069

Edward Woodward
Ravens Court
Calstock, Cornwall
PL18 9ST ENGLAND

Joanne Woodward
1120 - 5th Avenue #1C
New York, NY 10128

Y   Y

Amy Yasbeck
151 El Camino Drive
Beverly Hills, CA 90212

Michelle Yeoh
10301 West Pico Blvd., #121
Los Angeles, CA 90064

Robert Young
31589 Saddletree Drive
Westlake Village, CA 91361

Sean Young
P.O. Box 20547
Sedona, AZ 86341

Z   Z

Grace Zabriskie
1800 S. Robertson Blvd. #426
Los Angeles, CA 90035

Anthony Zerbe
1175 High Road
Santa Barbara, CA 93150

Pia Zadora
9560 Wilshire Blvd.
Beverly Hills, CA 90212

Ian Ziering
2700 Jalmia Drive
West Hollywood, CA 90046

Paula Zahn
524 West 57th Street
New York, NY 10019

Efrem Zimbalist, Jr.
1448 Holsted Drive
Solvang, CA 93463

Steve Zahn
2372 Veteran Avenue #102
Los Angeles, CA 90064

Stephanie Zimbalist
16255 Ventura Blvd. #1011
Encino, CA 91436

Roxana Zal
1450 Belfast Drive
Los Angeles, CA 90069

Kim Zimmer
9255 Sunset Blvd., #710
Los Angeles, CA 90069

Billy Zane
450 N. Rossmore Avenue #1001
Los Angeles, CA 90004

Adrian Zmed
4345 Freedom Drive, Unit E
Calabasas, CA 91302

Carmen Zapata
6107 Ethel Avenue
Van Nuys, CA 91405

Daphne Zuniga
P.O. Box 1249
White River Junction, VT 05001

Music

They're Not A Star Until
They're A Star In Star Guide™

A _____ A

Aaliyah
9255 Sunset Blvd., #804
West Hollywood, CA 90069

Paula Abdul
771 Teakwood Road
Los Angeles, CA 90049

AC/DC
46 Kensington Ct. St.
London W8 5DP ENGLAND

Bryan Adams
406 - 68 Water Street
Vancouver, BC, V6B 1A4 CANADA

ADC Band
17397 Santa Barbara
Detroit, MI 48221

Tracee Adkins
1250 - 6th Avenue #401
Santa Monica, CA 90401

Aerosmith
584 Broadway #1009
New York, NY 10012

Air Supply
14755 Ventura Blvd. #1-710
Sherman Oaks, CA 91403

Alabama
P.O. Box 529
Ft. Payne, AL 35967

Brick Alan
976 Murfreesboro Road, #93
Nashville, TN 37217

Alice In Chains
207 1/2 First Avenue So., #300
Seattle, WA 98104

Mose Allison
34 Dogwood Street
Smithtown, NY 11787

Greg Allman
650 California Street, #900
San Francisco, CA 94108

America
345 N. Maple Drive, #300
Beverly Hills, CA 90210

Tori Amos
P.O. Box 8456
Clearwater, FL 34618

Lynn Anderson
514 Fairlane Drive
Nashville, TN 37211

Julie Andrews
P.O. Box 491668
Los Angeles, CA 90049

Patti Andrews
9823 Aldea Avenue
Northridge, CA 91354

Paul Anka
10573 W. Pico Blvd., #159
Los Angeles, CA 90064

Adam Ant
503 The Chambers
Chelsea Harbour, Lots Road
London SW10 OXF ENGLAND

Ray Anthony
9288 Kinglet Drive
Los Angeles, CA 90069

Arrested Development
9380 SW 72nd Street #B-220
Miami, FL 33174

Ashford & Simpson
254 W. 72nd Street #1A
New York, NY 10023

Vladimir Ashkenazv
Sonnenhof 4
6004, Lucerne, SWITZERLAND

Asleep At The Wheel
P.O. Box 463
Austin, TX 75767

Frankie Avalon
4303 Spring Forest Lane
Westlake Village, CA 91362

Hoyt Axton
102 Bedford Street, #102
Hamilton, MT 59840

Charles Aznavour
76-78 ave. des Champs Elysses
F-75008 Paris FRANCE

B   B

B-52's
P.O. Box 60468
Rochester, NY 14606

Babyface
8436 West 3rd Street #650
Los Angeles, CA 90048

Burt Bacharach
10 Ocean Park Blvd. #4
Santa Monica, CA 90405

Joan Baez
P.O. Box 1026
Menlo Park, CA 94026

Anita Baker
8216 Tivoli Cove Drive
Las Vegas, NV 89128

Hank Ballard
P.O. Box 3125
Beverly Hills, CA 90212

Kaye Ballard
P.O. Box 922
Rancho Mirage, CA 92270

Shirley Bassey
24 Avenue Princess Grace #1200
Monte Carlo MONACO

Kathleen Battle
165 West 57th Street
New York, NY 10019

Bay City Rollers
27 Preston Grange
Road Preston Pans. East
Lothian, SCOTLAND

Beach Boys
4860 San Jacinto Circle #F
Fallbrook, CA 92028

Beastie Boys
c/o William Morris
1325 Avenue of the Stars
New York, NY 10019

Beavis & Butt-Head
1515 Braodway #400
New York, NY 10036

Beck
1325 Avenue of the Americas
New York, NY 10019

The Bee-Gees
20505 US 19 North #12-290
Clearwater, FL 34624

Harry Belafonte
300 West End Avenue, #5A
New York, NY 10023

Archie Bell
P.O. Box 11669
Knoxville, TN 37939

Bell Biv Devoe
P.O. Box 604
San Francisco, CA 94101

Bellamy Brothers
13917 Restless Lane
Dade City, FL 33525

Pat Benatar
2644 - 30th Street
Santa Monica, CA 90403

Tony Bennett
130 West 57th Street #9D
New York, NY 10019

Joan Benoit
RR #1, Box 1455AA
Freeport, ME 04302

George Benson
519 Next Day Hill Drive
Englewood, NJ 07631

Chuck Berry
Buckner Road - Berry Park
Wentzville, MO 63385

Clint Black
6255 Sunset Blvd., #1111
Hollywood, CA 90028

Black Oak Arkansas
1487 Red Fox Run
Lilburn, GA 30247

Mary J. Blige
40 West 57th Street
New York, NY 10019

Blood, Sweat & Tears
43 Washington Street
Groveland, MA 01834

Blur
20 Manchester Square
London W1A 1ES ENGLAND

Suzy Bogguss
33 Music Square W., #110
Nashville, TN 37203

Michael Bolton
P.O. Box 679
Branford, CT 06516

Jon Bon Jovi
250 W. 57th Street, #603
New York, NY 10107

Gary "US" Bonds
2011 Ferry Avenue #U-19
Camden, NJ 08104

Debbie Boone
4334 Kester Avenue
Sherman Oaks, CA 91403

Pat Boone
904 N. Beverly Drive
Beverly Hills, CA 90210

Victor Borge
Fieldpoint Park
Greenwich, CT 06830

David Bowie
55 Fulham High Street
London SW6 3JJ ENGLAND

Boxcar Willie
199 E. Garfield Road
Aurora, OH 44202

Boyz II Men
5750 Wilshire Blvd., #300
Los Angeles, CA 90036

Toni Braxton
3350 Peachtree Road #1500
Atlanta, GA 30326

Garth Brooks
3322 West End Avenue #1100
Nashville, TN 37203

James Brown
1217 West Medical Park Road
Augusta, GA 30909

T. Graham Brown
P.O. Box 50337
Nashville, TN 37205

Jackson Browne
3746 Kling Street
Studio City, CA 91604

Dave Brubeck
221 Millstone Road
Wilton, CT 06897

Lindsey Buckingham
900 Airole Way
Los Angeles, CA 90077

Jimmy Buffett
424A Fleming Street
Key West, FL 33040

Bush
10900 Wilshire Blvd., #1230
Los Angeles, CA 90024

C   C

Glen Campbell
28 Biltmore Est.
Phoenix, AZ 85016

Luther Campbell
8400 N.E. 2nd Avenue
Miami, FL 33138

Freddie Cannon
18641 Cassandra Street
Tarzana, CA 91356

Irene Cara
8033 Sunset Blvd., #735
Los Angeles, CA 90046

Mariah Carey
P.O. Box 4450
New York, NY 10101

Belinda Carlisle
21A Noel Street
London WIV 3PDD ENGLAND

Kim Carnes
2031 Old Natchez Terrace
Franklin, TN 37064

Mary-Chapin Carpenter
1250-6th Street #401
Santa Monica, CA 90401

Richard Carpenter
9386 Raviller Drive
Downey, CA 90240

Vikki Carr
P.O. Box 780968
San Antonio, TX 78278

Betty Carter
307 Lake Street
San Francisco, CA 94118

Carlene Carter
50 W. Main Street
Ventura, CA 93001

Deana Carter
9830 Wilshire Blvd.
Beverly Hills, CA 90212

Johnny Cash
700 E. Main Street
Hendersonville, TN 37075

David Cassidy
3799 Las Vegas Blvd. South
Las Vegas, NV 89109

Shaun Cassidy
8484 Wilshire Blvd., #500
Beverly Hills, CA 90212

Peter Cetera
1880 Century Park East #900
Los Angeles, CA 90067

Ray Charles
2107 W. Washington Blvd., #200
Los Angeles, CA 90018

Chubby Checker
320 Fayette Street #200
Conshohocken, PA 19426

Cher
P.O. Box 960
Beverly Hills, CA 90213

Mark Chestnut
P.O. Box 128031
Nashville, TN 37212

Eric Clapton
46 Kensington Court
London WE8 5DP ENGLAND

Dick Clark
3003 W. Olive Avenue
Burbank, CA 91505

Roy Clark
1800 Forrest Blvd.
Tulsa, OK 74114

Van Cliburn
455 Wilder Place
Shreveport, LA 71104

Rosemary Clooney
1019 N. Roxbury Drive
Beverly Hills, CA 90210

The Coasters
4905 S. Atlantic Avenue
Daytona Beach, FL 32127

Iron Eyes Cody
2013 Griffith Park Blvd.
Los Angeles, CA 90039

Natalie Cole
955 South Carrillo Drive #200
Los Angeles, CA 90048

Mark Collie
3322 West End Avenue #520
Nashville, TN 37203

Judy Collins
450-7th Avenue #603
New York, NY 10123

Phil Collins
30 Ives Street
London SW3 2ND ENGLAND

Jessie Colter
1117 - 17th Avenue South
Nashville, TN 37212

Sean "Puff Daddy" Combs
8436 West 3rd Street #650
Los Angeles, CA 90048

Perry Como
305 Northern Blvd. #3A
Great Neck, NY 11021

Harry Connick, Jr.
323 Broadway
Cambridge, MA 02139

Rita Coolidge
560 Hibert Drive
Fallbrook, CA 92028

Alice Cooper
4135 E. Keim Street
Paradise Valley, AZ 85253

Chick Corea
2635 Griffith Park Blvd.
Los Angeles, CA 90039

Christopher Cross
P.O. Box 127465
Nashville, TN 37212

Elvis Costello
9028 Great Guest Road
Middlesex TW8 9EW, ENGLAND

Sheryl Crow
10345 W. Olympic Blvd., #200
Los Angeles, CA 90064

Billy "Crash" Craddock
3007 Old Martinsville Road
Greensboro, NC 27455

Rodney Crowell
P.O. Box 120576
Nashville, TN 37212

David Crosby
P.O. Box 9008
Solvang, CA 93464

Cherie Currie
3050 N. Chandelle Road
Los Angeles, CA 90046

Crosby, Stills, & Nash
14930 Ventura Blvd., #206
Sherman Oaks, CA 91403

Billy Ray Cyrus
1225-B 16th Avenue
Nashville, TN 38212

D   D

Roger Daltry
18/21 Jermyn Street #300
London SW1Y 6HP ENGLAND

John Davidson
6051 Spring Valley Road
Hidden Hills, CA 91302

Vic Damone
21700 Oxnard Street #400
Woodland Hills, CA 91367

Jimmy Dean
8000 Centerview Parkway #400
Cordova, TN 38018

Charlie Daniels Band
17060 Central Pike
Lebanon, TX 37087

Deep Purple
P.O. Box 254
Sheffield S6 IDF ENGLAND

Terence Trent D'Arby
10 Great Marlborough Street
London W1V 2LP ENGLAND

Rick Dees
3400 Riverside Dr., #800
Burbank, CA 91505

Def Leppard
72 Chancellor's Road
London W6 9QB ENGLAND

Suzanne DePasse
1100 North Alta Loma #805
Los Angeles, CA 90069

Depeche Mode
P.O. Box 1281
London, N1 9UX, ENGLAND

Neil Diamond
10345 W. Olympic Blvd., #200
Los Angeles, CA 90064

Diamond Rio
242 W. Main Street #236
Hendersonville, TN 37075

Bo Diddley
1560 Broadway, #1308
New York, NY 10036

Joe Diffie
1009 - 16th Avenue South
Nashville, TN 37212

Celine Dion
4 Place Laval #500
Laval, PQQ H7N 5Y3 CANADA

Dire Straits
509 Hartnell Street
Monterey, CA 93940

Mickey Dolenz
9000 Sunset Blvd. #1200
Los Angeles, CA 90069

Placido Domingo
150 Central Park South
New York, NY 10019

Fats Domino
5515 Marais Street
New Orleans, LA 70117

Doobie Brothers
15140 Sonoma Hwy.
Glen Ellen, CA 95442

The Doors
144 South Elm Drive #5
Beverly Hills, CA 90212

The Drifters
10 Chelsea Court
Neptune, NJ 07753

Peter Duchin
305 Madison Avenue #956
New York, NY 10165

Sandy Duncan
61 West 90th Street
New York, NY 10024

Holly Dunn
209 10th Avenue So., #347
Nashville, TN 37203

Duran Duran
P.O. Box 21
London, W10 6XA, ENGLAND

Bob Dylan
P.O. Box 870, Cooper Station
New York, NY 10276

81

E   E

Duane Eddy
1906 Chet Atkins Plaza #502
Nashville, TN 37212

Electric Light Orchestra
9850 Sandalfoot Blvd., #458
Boca Raton, FL 33428

Larry Elgart
2065 Gulf Of Mexico Drive
Longboat Key, FL 34228

En Vogue
151 El Camino
Beverly Hills, CA 90212

John Entwhistle
1705 Queen Court
Los Angeles, CA 90068

Gloria Estefan
555 Jefferson Avenue
Miami Beach, FL 33139

Melissa Etheridge
P.O. Box 884563
San Francisco, CA 94188

Kevin Eubanks
173 Brighton Avenue
Boston, MA 02134

Everly Brothers
277 Comroe Road
Nashville, TN 37211

Extreme
189 Carlton Street
Toronto, Ontario
M5A 2K7 CANADA

F   F

Faith No More
5550 Wilshire Blvd., #202
Los Angeles, CA 90036

Marianne Faithfull
235 Footscray Road
New Eltham
Londaon SE9 2El ENGLAND

Lola Falana
1201 "N" Street, NW #A-5
Washington DC 20005

Donna Fargo
P.O. Box 150527
Nashville, TN 37215

Fat Boys
250 W. 57th Street, #1723
New York, NY 10107

Dr. Feelgood
3 E. 54th Street
New York, NY 10022

Jose Feliciano
266 Lyons Plain Road
Weston, CT 06883

Freddy Fender
P.O. Box 270540
Corpus Christi, TX 78427

Maynard Ferguson
P.O. Box 716
Ojai, CA 93023

Ferrante & Teicher
12224 Avila Drive
Kansas City, MO 64145

The Firm
57A Great Titchfield Street
London, W1P 7FL, ENGLAND

Eddie Fisher
10000 North Point Street #1802
San Francisco, CA 94109

Roberta Flack
1 West 72nd Street
New York, NY 10023

Flash Cadillac
433 E. Cucharras Street
Colorado Springs, CO 80903

Mick Fleetwood
4905 S. Atlantic Avenue
Daytona Beach, FL 32127

Myron Floren
26 Georgeff Road
Rolling Hills, CA 90274

Dan Fogelberg
P.O. Box 2399
Pagosa Springs, CO 81147

Foreigner
9830 Wilshire Blvd.
Beverly Hills, CA 90212

Forester Sisters
P.O. Box 1456
Trenton, GA 30752

Pete Fountain
237 North Peters Street #400
New Orleans, LA 71030

The Four Seasons
P.O. Box 262
Carteret, NJ 07008

Peter Frampton
8927 Byron Avenue
Surfside, FL 33154

Connie Francis
50 Sullivan Drive
West Orange, NJ 07052

Aretha Franklin
16919 Stansbury
Detroit, MI 48235

Glen Frey
8900 Wilshire Blvd., #300
Beverly Hills, CA 90211

Janie Fricke
P.O. Box 798
Lancaster, TX 75146

G   G

Kenny G
3500 W. Olive Avenue #680
Burbank, CA 91505

Art Garfunkel
9 East 79th Street
New York, NY 10021

Larry Gatlin
Fantasy Harbour, Waccamaw
Myrtle Beach, SC 29577

Crystal Gayle
51 Music Square East
Nashville, TN 37203

Gloria Gaynor
Longford Avenue
Southall
Middlesex UB1 3QT ENGLAND

David Geffen
P.O. Box 8520
Universal City, CA 91608

Sir Bob Geldof
Davington Priory, Faversham
Kent, ENGLAND

Genesis
25 Ives Street
London, SW3, ENGLAND

Bobby Gentry
8 Tidewater Way
Savannah, GA 31411

Barry Gibb
29505 US 19 North #12-290
Clearwater, FL 34624

Debbie Gibson
300 Main Street #201
Huntington, NY 11743

Johnny Gill
17539 Corinthian Drive
Encino, CA 91316

Vince Gill
P.O. Box 1407
White House, TN 37188

Mickey Gilley
P.O. Box 1242
Pasadena, TX 77501

Philip Glass
231 - 2nd Avenue
New York, NY 10003

Bobby Goldsboro
P.O. Box 5250
Ocala, FL 32678

Berry Gordy
878 Stradella Road
Los Angeles, CA 90077

Lesley Gore
170 E. 77th Street #2A
New York, NY 10021

Eydie Gorme
820 Greenway Drive
Beverly Hills, CA 90210

Robert Goulet
3110 Monte Rosa
Las Vegas, NV 89120

Amy Grant
2910 Poston Avenue
Nashville, TN 37203

Rev. Al Green
P.O. Box 456
Millington, TN 38083

Green Day
9830 Wilshire Blvd.
Beverly Hills, CA 90212

Lee Greenwood
P.O. Box 6537
Sevierville, TN 37864

Guns & Roses
83 Riverside Drive
New York, NY 10024

Arlo Guthrie
The Farm
Washington, MA 01223

H   H

Sammy Hagar
8502 Fathom Drive
Baldwinsville, CA 13027

Merle Haggard
3009 East Street
Sevierville, TN 37862

Tom T. Hall
P.O. Box 1246
Franklin, TN 37065

Marvin Hamlisch
970 Park Avenue #501
New York, NY 10028

Lionel Hampton
44 Rio Vista Drive
Allendale, NJ 07401

Herbie Hancock
3 East 28th Street #600
New York, NY 10016

EmmyLou Harris
P.O. Box 158568
Nashville, TN 37215

George Harrison
5 Friar Park Road
Henly-On-Thames, ENGLAND

Deborah Harry
156 W. 56th Street, Fifth Floor
New York, NY 10019

Corey Hart
81 Hymus Blvd.
Montreal, PQ Que. H9R 1E2
CANADA

Richie Havens
123 West 44th Street #11A
New York, NY 10036

Hootie & the Blowfish
917 Huger Street
Columbia, SC 29201

Edwin Hawkins
2041 Locust Street
Philadelphia, PA 19103

Telma Hopkins
4122 Don Luis Drive
Los Angeles, CA 90008

Isaac Hayes
504 W. 168th Street
New York, NY 10032

Lena Horne
23 East 74th Street
New York, NY 10021

Heart
151 El Camino Drive
Beverly Hills, CA 90212

Marilyn Horne
165 West 57th Street
New York, NY 10019

Don Henley
8942 Wilshire Blvd.
Beverly Hills, CA 90211

Bruce Hornsby
P.O. Box 3545
Williamsburg, VA 23187

Faith Hill
480 Glen Arbor Circle
Cordova, TN 37018

Thelma Houston
4296 Mt. Vernon
Los Angeles, CA 90008

Al Hirt
3530 Rue Delphine
New Orleans, LA 70131

Whitney Houston
2160 N. Central Road
Ft. Lee, NJ 07024

John Lee Hooker
P.O. Box 170429
San Francisco, CA 94117

Englebert Humperdinck
10100 Sunset Blvd.
Los Angeles, CA 90077

I   I

Ice Cube
2155 Van Wick Street
Los Angeles, CA 90047

Ice-Tea
2287 Sunset Plaza Drive
Los Angeles, CA 90069

Billy Idol
7314 Woodrow Wilson Drive
Los Angeles, CA 90046

Julio Iglesias
5 Indian Creek Drive
Miami, FL 33154

Indigo Girls
315 Ponce De Leon Avenue #755
Decatur, GA 30030

The Isley Brothers
4229 Montieth Drive
Los Angeles, CA 90043

J _____ J

Alan Jackson
1101-17th Avenue South
Nashville, TN 37212

Freddie Jackson
231 W. 58th Street
New York, NY 10019

Janet Jackson
14755 Ventura Blvd. #1-170
Sherman Oaks, CA 91403

Jermaine Jackson
4641 Hayvenhurst Avenue
Encino, CA 91316

Joe Jackson
6 Pembridge Road
Trinity House #200
London, W11, ENGLAND

Marlon Jackson
4641 Hayvenhurst Avenue
Encino, CA 91316

Michael Jackson
Neverland Ranch
Los Olivos, CA 93441

Tito Jackson
23726 Long Valley Road
Hidden Hills, CA 91302

Mick Jagger
304 West 81st Street
New York, NY 10024

Etta James
16409 Sally Lane
Riverside, CA 92504

Janes's Addiction
8800 Sunset Blvd. #401
Los Angeles, CA 90069

Al Jarreau
29171 Grayfox Street
Malibu, CA 90265

Waylon Jennings
824 Old Hickory Blvd.
Brentwood, TN 37027

Jethro Tull
2 Wansdown Pl., Fulham
London SW6 ENGLAND

Joan Jett
155 E. 55th Street, #6H
New York, NY 10022

Rickie Lee Jones
476 Broome Street #6A
New York, NY 10013

Jewel
P.O. Box 33494
San Diego, CA 92163

Tom Jones
4130 Stansbury Avenue
Sherman Oaks, CA 91403

Billy Joel
280 Elm Street
Southampton, NY 11968

Montel Jordan
250 West 57th Street #821
New York, NY 10107

Sir Elton John
Woodside, Crump Hill Road
Old Windsor, Berkshire ENGLAND

Journey
650 California Street #900
San Francisco, CA 94108

Davey Jones
P.O. Box 400
Beavertown, PA 17813

Ashley Judd
P.O. Box 680339
Franklin, TN 37068

Quincy Jones
3800 Barham Blvd. #503
Los Angeles, CA 90068

Naomi Judd
P.O. Box 682068
Franklin, TN 37068

K   K

K.C. & the Sunshine Band
4770 Biscayne Blvd., PH
Miami, FL 33137

Chaka Khan
P.O. Box 16680
Beverly Hills, CA 90209

Casey Kasem
138 N. Mapleton Drive
Los Angeles, CA 90077

B.B. King
1414 Sixth Avenue
New York, NY 10019

Hal Ketchum
1700 Hayes Street #304
Nashville, TN 37203

Ben E. King
P.O. Box 1094
Teaneck, NJ 07666

Carole King
509 Hartnell Street
Monterey, CA 93940

Kiss
8730 Sunset Blvd., #175
Los Angeles , CA 90069

Gladys Knight
2801 Yorkshire Avenue
Henderson, NV 89014

Mark Knopfler
16 Lamberton Plaza
London W11 2SH ENGLAND

Kool & The Gang
89 Fifth Avenue, #700
New York, NY 10003

Alison Krauss
1017-16th Avenue South
Nashville, TN 37212

Lenny Kravitz
14681 Harrison Street
Miami, FL 33176

Kris Kristofferson
P.O. Box 2147
Malibu, CA 90265

L _____ **L**

Patti LaBelle
1212 Grennox Road
Wynnewood, PA 19096

K.D. Lang
Box 33800, Station D
Vancouver B.C.
V6J 5C7 CANADA

Cyndi Lauper
826 Broadway #400
New York, NY 10003

Tracy Lawrence
2100 West End Avenue #1000
Nashville, TN 37203

Chris Ledoux
4205 Hillsboro Road #208
Nashville, TN 37215

Brenda Lee
26 Fall Creek Drive #6
Branson, MO 65616

Julian Lennon
30 Ives Street
London, SW3 2ND ENGLAND

Sean Lennon
1 W. 72nd Street
New York, NY 10023

LeVert
110 - 112 Lantoga Road #D
Wayne, PA 19087

Huey Lewis
P.O. Box 779
Mill Valley, CA 94942

Jerry Lee Lewis
P.O. Box 23162
Nashville, TN 37202

Gordon Lightfoot
1365 Yonge Street #207
Toronto, Ont. M4T 2P7 CANADA

LL Cool J
160 Varick Street
New York, NY 10013

Kenny Loggins
670 Oak Springs Lane
Santa Barbara, CA 93108

Lost Boys
1775 Broadway #433
New York, NY 10019

Courtney Love
9072 Wonderland Park Avenue
Los Angeles, CA 90046

Patty Loveless
P.O. Box 1407
White House, TN 37188

Lyle Lovett
c/o General Delivery
Klein, TX 77391

Loretta Lynn
P.O. Box 120369
Nashville, TN 37212

Lynyrd Skynyrd
3423 Piedmont Road NE, #220
Atlanta, GA 30305

M   M

Madonna
4519 Cockerham Drive
Los Angeles, CA 90027

Taj Mahal
1671 Appian Way
Santa Monica, CA 90401

The Mamas & The Papas
108 E. Matilija Street
Ojai, CA 93023

Melissa Manchester
15822 High Knoll Road
Encino, CA 91436

Barbara Mandrell
605-C N. Main Street
Ashland City, TN 37015

Erline Mandrell
605-C N. Main Street
Ashland City, TN 37015

Louise Mandrell
2046 Parkway
Pigeon Forge, TN 37863

Barry Manilow
5443 Beethoven Street
Los Angeles, CA 90066

Marilyn Manson
83 Riverside Drive
New York, NY 10024

Marky Mark
63 Pilgrim Road
Braintree, MA 02184

Ziggy Marley
Jack's Hill
Kingston, JAMAICA

Branford Marsalis
3 Hastings Square
Cambridge, MA 02139

Wynton Marsalis
3 Lincoln Center #2911
New York, NY 10023

Richard Marx
15250 Ventura Blvd. #900
Sherman Oaks, CA 91403

Johnny Mathis
3500 W. Olive Avenue #750
Burbank, CA 91505

Sir Paul McCartney
1 Soho Square
London, WI ENGLAND

Marilyn McCoo
2639 Lavery Court #5
Newbury Park, CA 91320

"Country Joe" McDonald
P.O. Box 7064
Berkeley, CA 94707

Reba McEntyre
40 Music Square West
Nashville, TN 37203

Bobby McFerrin
826 Broadway, #400
New York, NY 10003

Maureen McGovern
163 Amsterdam Avenue, #174
New York, NY 10023

Tim McGraw
3310 West End Avenue #500
Nashville, TN 37203

The McGuire Sisters
100 Rancho Circle
Las Vegas, NV 89119

Zubin Mehta
27 Oakmont Drive
Los Angeles, CA 90049

John Mellencamp
Rt. 1, Box 361
Nashville, IN 47448

Sergio Mendez
4849 Encino Avenue
Encino, CA 91316

Menudo
2895 Biscayne Blvd., #455
Miami, FL 33137

Sir Yehudi Menuhin
Buhlstr
CH-3780 Gstaad-Neueret
SWITZERLAND

Metallica
729 7th Avenue, #1400
New York, Ny 10019

George Michael
338 N. Foothill Road
Beverly Hills, CA 90210

Bette Midler
135 Watts Street #400
New York, NY 10013

Mitch Miller
345 W. 58th Street
New York, NY 10019

Stephanie Mills
1995 Broadway #501
New York, NY 10023

Ronnie Milsap
3015 Theater Drive
Myrtle Beach, SC 29577

Charles Mingus
484 West 43rd Street #43-S
New York, NY 10036

Liza Minnelli
160 Central Park South
New York, NY 10019

Joni Mitchell
1505 West 2nd Avenue #200
Vancouver BC V6H 3Y4 CANADA

Eddie Money
P.O. Box 429094
San Francisco, CA 94142

Lorrie Morgan
P.O. Box 78
Spencer, TN 37212

Alanis Morissette
75 Rockefeller Plaza #2100
New York, NY 10019

Van Morrison
12304 Santa Monica Blvd. #300
Los Angeles, CA 90025

Motley Crue
6255 Sunset Blvd., #1111
Hollywood, CA 90028

Maria Muldaur
311 Oakdale Road
Charlotte, NC 28216

Anne Murray
406-68 Water Street
Vancouver BC V6B 14A CANADA

N _____ N

Graham Nash
14930 Ventura Blvd., #205
Sherman Oaks, CA 91403

Naughty by Nature
155 Morgan Street
Jersey City, NJ 07302

Willie Nelson
Rt. #1, Briarcliff TT
Spicewood, TX 78669

Peter Nero
11806 N. 56th Street #B
Tampa, FL 33617

Michael Nesmith
2828 Donald Douglas Loop N. #15
Santa Monica, CA 90405

Aaron Neville
P.O. Box 750187
New Orleans, LA 70130

New Kids on the Block
27 Dudley Street
Roxbury, MA 02132

Tommy Newsom
19315 Wells Drive
Tarzana, CA 91356

Juice Newton
P.O. Box 3035
Rancho Santa Fe, CA 92067

Wayne Newton
3422 Happy Lane
Las Vegas, NV 89120

Olivia Newton-John
P.O. Box 2710
Malibu, CA 90265

Stevie Nicks
P.O. Box 7855
Alhambra, CA 91802

Nirvana
151 El Camino Drive
Beverly Hills, CA 90212

Ted Nugent
8000 Eckert
Concord, MI 49237

O   O

Oak Ridge Boys
2102 W. Linden Avenue
Nashville, TN 37212

Sinead O'Connor
3 East 54th Street #500
New York, NY 10022

The O'Jays
1995 Broadway #501
New York, NY 10023

Mike Oldfield
115-A Glenthorne Road
London W6 0LJ ENGLAND

Yoko Ono (Lennon)
One W. 72nd Street
New York, NY 10023

Tony Orlando
3220 Falls Parkway
Branson, MO 65616

Ozzy Osbourne
9 Highpoint Drive
Gulf Breeze, FL 32561

Marie Osmond
3325 North University Avenue
Provo, UT 84604

K. T. Oslin
1103 - 16th Avenue
Nashville, TN 37212

Paul Overstreet
909 Meadowlark Lane
Goodletteville, TN 37072

Donny Osmond
36 Avignon
Newport Beach, CA 92657

Buck Owens
3223 Sillect Avenue
Bakersfield, CA 93308

P   P

Pablo Cruise
P.O. Box 779
Mill Valley, CA 94941

Johnny Paycheck
P.O. Box 916
Hendersonville, TN 37077

Patti Page
71537 Hwy. 111 #K
Rancho Mirage, CA 92270

Peaches & Herb
7319-C Hanover Parkway
Greenbelt, MD 20770

Robert Palmer
584 Broadway #1201
New York, NY 10012

Pearl Jam
417 Denny Way, #200
Seattle, WA 98109

Dolly Parton
P.O. Box 150307
Nashville, TN 37215

Teddy Pendergrass
1505 Flat Rock Road
Narberth, PA 19072

Les Paul
78 Deerhaven Road
Mahwah, NJ 07430

The Penguins
708 West 137th Street
Gardena, CA 90247

Luciano Pavarotti
Via Giardini
I-41040 Saliceto
Panaro, ITALY

The Persuaders
225 West 57th Street #500
New York, NY 10019

Peter, Paul & Mary
121 Mt. Herman Way
Ocean Grove, NJ 07756

Oscar Peterson
2421 Hammond Road
Mississagua, Ont. L5K 1T3 CANADA

Tom Petty
4626 Encino Avenue
Encino, CA 91316

Michelle Phillips
P.O. Box 67758
Beverly Hills, CA 90209

Sam Phillips
639 Madison Avenue
Memphis, TN 38103

Wilson Pickett
102 Ryders Lane
East Brunswick, NJ 08816

Ray Pillow
2802 Columbine Plaza
Nashville, TN 37204

Pink Floyd
43 Portland Road
London, W11 ENGLAND

The Platters
2756 N. Green Valley Parkway #449
Las Vegas, NV 89014

Pointer Sisters
1900 Avenue of the Stars #1640
Los Angeles, CA 90067

Poison
1750 North Vine Street
Hollywood, CA 90028

The Police
194 Kensington Park Road
London, W11 2ES, ENGLAND

Iggy Pop
P.O. Box 561
Pine Bush, NY 12565

Billy Preston
4271 Garthwaite Avenue
Los Angeles, CA 90008

Andre Previn
8 Sherwood Lane
Bedford Hills, NY 10507

Leontyne Price
9 Van Dam Street
New York, NY 10003

Charlie Pride
P.O. Box 670507
Dallas, TX 75367

Prince (formely known)
9401 Kiowa Trail
Chanhassen, MN 55317

Gary Puckett
11088 Indian Lore Court
San Diego, CA 92127

Public Enemy
298 Elizabeth Street
New York, NY 10012

Q   Q

Queen
16A High Street Barnes
London SW13 9LW ENGLAND

Quiet Riot
P.O. Box 24455
New Orleans, LA 70184

R   R

Bonnie Raitt
1344 N. Spaulding
Los Angeles, CA 90046

R.E.M.
P.O. Box 128288
Nashville, TN 37212

Eddy Raven
1071 Bradley Road
Gallatin, TN 37066

Paul Revere and the Raiders
P.O. Box 544
Grangeville, ID 83530

Lou Rawls
109 Fremont Place
Los Angeles, CA 90005

Sir Cliff Richard
Portsmouth Road
Box 46A, Esher
Surrey KT10 9AA ENGLAND

Red Hot Chili Peppers
11116 Aqua Vista #39
North Hollywood, CA 91602

Little Richard (Penniman)
Hyatt Sunset Hotel
8401 Sunset Blvd
Los Angeles, CA 90069

Helen Reddy
820 Stanford
Santa Monica, CA 90403

Keith Richards
"Redlands"
West Wittering
Chichester, Sussex, ENGLAND

Lou Reed
250 West 57th Street #620
New York, NY 10107

Lionel Richie
P.O. Box 9055
Calabasas, CA 91372

Martha Reeves
P.O. Box 1987
Paramount, CA 90723

Righteous Brothers
9841 Hot Springs Drive
Huntington Beach, CA 92646

Jeannie C. Riley
105 Ewingville Drive
Franklin, TN 37064

LeAnn Rimes
1801 Whitehall Lane
Garland, TX 75043

Smokey Robinson
17085 Rancho Street
Encino, CA 91316

Johnny Rodriquez
P.O. Box 23162
Nashville, TN 37202

Kenny Rogers
P.O. Box 24240
Nashville, TN 37202

Rolling Stones
P.O. Box 6152
New York, NY 10128

Sonny Rollins
193 Brighton Avenue
Boston, MA 02134

Linda Ronstadt
644 North Doheny
Los Angeles, CA 90069

Axl Rose
9229 Sunset Blvd., #607
Los Angeles, CA 90069

Rosemarie
6916 Chisholm Avenue
Van Nuys, CA 91406

Diana Ross
Box 11059, Glenville Station
Greenwich, CT 06831

David Lee Roth
455 Bradford Street
Pasadena, CA 91105

Billy Joe Royal
P.O. Box 50572
Nashville, TN 37205

Run-D.M.C.
160 Varick Street
New York, NY 10013

Rupaul
6671 Sunset Blvd. #1590
Hollywood, CA 90028

Bobby Rydell
917 Bryn Mawr Avenue
Narberth, PA 19072

S   S

Sade
10 Great Marlborough Street
London W1V 2LP ENGLAND

Carole Bayer Sager
10761 Bellagio Road
Los Angeles, CA 90077

Buffy Sainte-Marie
20 Duncan Street #200
Toronto, Ont. M5H 3G8 CANADA

Salt & Pepper
1700 Broadway #500
New York, NY 10019

Carlos Santana
P.O. Box 10348
San Rafael, CA 94912

Boz Scaggs
8900 Wilshire Blvd. #300
Beverly Hills, CA 90211

Lalo Schifrin
710 N. Hillcrest Road
Beverly Hills, CA 90210

Earl Scruggs
P.O. Box 66
Madison, TN 37115

Seal
56 Beethoven Street
London W10 4LG ENGLAND

John Sebastian
3520 Hayden Avenue
Culver City, CA 90232

Jon Secada
601 Brickell Key Drive #200
Miami, FL 33131

Neil Sedaka
888 - 7th Avenue #1600
New York, NY 10106

Pete Seeger
Duchess Junction, Box 431
Beacon, NY 12508

Bob Seger
567 Purdy
Birmingham, MI 48009

Doc Severinsen
4275 White Pine Lane
Santa Ynez, CA 93460

Sha Na Na
1720 N. Ross Street
Santa Ana, CA 92706

Paul Shaffer
1697 Broadway
New York, NY 10019

Shanice
8455 Fountain Avenue #530
Los Angeles, CA 90069

Artie Shaw
2127 W. Palos Court
Newbury Park, CA 91320

Tommy Shaw
6025 The Comers Parkway #202
Norcross, GA 30092

Shenandoah
1028-B 18th Avenue So.
Nashville, TN 37212

T. G. Sheppard
3341 Arlington Avenue #F-206
Toledo, OH 43614

Bobby Sherman
1870 Sunset Plaza Drive
Los Angeles, CA 90069

Beverly Sills
211 Central Park West #4F
New York, NY 10024

Gene Simmons
2650 Benedict Canyon
Beverly Hills, CA 90210

Paul Simon
110 W. 57th Street #300
New York, NY 10019

Nina Simone
7250 Franklin Avenue #115
New York, NY 10046

Frank Sinatra, Jr.
2211 Florian Place
Beverly Hills, CA 90210

Nancy Sinatra
P.O. Box 69453
Los Angeles, CA 90069

Tina Sinatra
30966 Broad Beach Road
Malibu, CA 90265

Sex Pistols
100 Wilshire Blvd. #1830
Santa Monica, CA 90401

Ricky Skaggs
380 Forest Retreat
Hendersonville, TN 37075

Grace Slick
5956 Kanan Dume Road
Malibu, CA 90265

Smashing Pumpkins
8380 Melrose Avenue, #210
Los Angeles, CA 90069

Vince Smith
P.O. Box 1221
Pottsville, PA 17901

Snoop Doggy Dog
10900 Wilshire Blvd. #1230
Los Angeles, CA 90024

Hank Snow
P.O. Box 1084
Nashville, TN 37202

Phil Spector
1210 South Arroyo Blvd.
Pasadena, CA 91101

Ronnie Spector
39B Mill Plan Road #233
Danbury, CT 06811

Spinal Tap
15250 Ventura Blvd., #1215
Sherman Oaks, CA 91403

Spice Girls
35-37 Parkgate Road Unit 32
Ransomes Dock
London SWII 4NP ENGLAND

Rick Springfield
P.O. Box 261640
Encino, CA 914726

Bruce Springsteen
1224 Benedict Canyon
Beverly Hills, CA 90210

Spyro Gyro
926 Horseshoe Road
Suffern, NY 10301

Billy Squier
P.O. Box 1251
New York, NY 10023

Lisa Stansfield
Box 59, Ashwall
Herfordshire SG7 5NG ENGLAND

Ringo Starr
1541 Ocean Avenue, #200
Santa Monica, CA 90401

Statler Brothers
P.O. Box Box 492
Hernando, MS 38632

Isaac Stern
211 Central Park West
New York, NY 10024

Connie Stevens
426 South Robertson Blvd.
Los Angeles, CA 90048

Ray Stevens
817 North 2nd Street
San Jose, CA 95112

Shadoe Stevens
2570 Benedict Canyon
Beverly Hills, CA 90210

Rod Stewart
3500 W. Olive Avenue #920
Burbank, CA 91505

Sting
2 The Grove,
Highgate Village
London, N6, ENGLAND

Sly Stone
6467 Sunset Blvd. #1110
Hollywood, CA 90028

George Strait
1000 18th Avenue South
Nashville, TN 37212

Barbra Streisand
301 North Carolwood
Los Angeles, CA 90077

Marty Stuart
119 W. 17th Avenue So.
Nashville, TN 37203

Donna Summer
18165 Eccles
Northridge, CA 91324

Joan Sutherland
c/o Colbert Artists
111 W. 57th Street
New York, NY 10019

Keith Sweat
40 West 57th Street
New York, NY 10019

SWV
35 Hart Street
Brooklyn, NY 11206

T   T

Bernie Taupin
450 North Maple Drive #501
Beverly Hills, CA 90210

James Taylor
644 N. Doheny Drive
Los Angeles, CA 90069

The Temptations
1325 Avenue of the Americas
New York, NY 10019

Toni Tennille
P.O. Box 608
Zephyr Cove, NV 89448

Clark Terry
24 Westland Drive
Glen Cove, NY 11542

B.J. Thomas
P.O.Box 1200003
Arlington, TX 76012

The Thompson Twins
9 Eccleston Street
London, SW1, ENGLAND

Hank Thompson
5 Rushing Creek Court
Roanoke, TX 76262

Three Degrees
19 The Willows
Maidenhead Road
Windsor, Berk, ENGLAND

Tiffany
13659 Victory Blvd., #550
Van Nuys, CA 91401

Mel Tillis
P.O. Box 1626
Branson, MO 65616

Pam Tillis
P.O. Box 128575
Nashville, TN 37212

Aaron Tippin
P.O. Box 41689
Nashville, TN 37204

Tony! Tony! Tony!
484 Lake Park Avenue #21
Oakland, CA 94610

Mel Torme
1734 Coldwater Canyon
Beverly Hills, CA 90210

Liz Torres
1206 Havenhurst Drive
Los Angeles, CA 90046

Toto
50 West Main Street
Ventura, CA 93001

Randy Travis
P.O. Box 121712
Nashville, TN 37212

Joey Travolta
4975 Chimineas Avenue
Tarzana, CA 91356

Travis Tritt
1112 N. Sherbourne Drive
Los Angeles, CA 90069

Marshall Tucker Band
315 S. Beverly Drive, #206
Beverly Hills, CA 90212

Tanya Tucker
901 - 6th Avenue South
Nashville, TN 37203

Tina Turner
3377 Fryman Place
Studio City, CA 91604

Stanley Turrentine
P.O. Box 44555
Ft. Washington, MD 20749

2 Live Crew
8400 N.E. 2nd Avenue
Miami, FL 33138

Bonnie Tyler
10 Great Marlborough Street
London W1V 2LP ENGLAND

U   U

U2
119 Rockland Center, Box 350
Nanuet, NY 10954

UFO
10 Sutherland
London W9 24Q ENGLAND

Leslie Uggams
3 Lincoln Center
New York, NY 10023

Tracey Ullman
815 East Colorado Street #210
Glendale, CA 91205

V   V

Jerry Vale
1100 N. Alta Loma Road, #1404
Los Angeles, CA 90069

Frankie Valli
6400 Pleasant Park Drive
Chanhassen, MN 55317

Richard Van Allen
18 Octavia Street
London, SW11 3DN, ENGLAND

Eddie Van Halen
3361 Coldwater Canyon
North Hollywood, CA 91604

Luther Vandross
3264 South Kihei Road
Kihei, HI 96753

Vanilla Ice
1290 Avenue of the Americas #4200
New York, NY 10104

Vanity
43521 Mission Blvd.
Fremont, CA 94539

Steve Van Zandt
322 West 57th Street
New York, NY 10019

Bobby Vee
P.O. Box 41
Sauk Rapids, MN 56379

Suzanne Vega
30 W. 21st Street, #700
New York, NY 10010

The Village People
1560 Broadway, #1308
New York, NY 10036

Bobby Vinton
P.O. Box 6010
Branson, MO 65616

W   W

Porter Wagoner
P.O. Box 290785
Nashville, TN 37229

Tom Waits
P.O. Box 498
Valley Ford, CA 94972

Clay Walker
1000-18th Avenue South
Nashville, TN 37212

Junior Walker
141 Dunbar Avenue
Fords, NJ 08863

Steve Wariner
320 Main Street #240
Franklin, TN 37064

Dionne Warwick
1583 Lindacrest Drive
Beverly Hills, CA 90210

Jody Watley
P.O. Box 6339
Beverly HIlls, CA 90212

Andre Watts
205 West 57th Street
New York, NY 10019

Kitty Wells
240 Old Hickory Blvd.
Madison, TN 35115

Barry White
3395 South Jones Blvd., #176
Las Vegas, NV 89102

Karyn White
3300 Warner Blvd.
Burbank, CA 91505

Thelma White
8431 Lennox Avenue
Panorama City, CA 91402

Slim Whitman
1300 Division Street #103
Nashville, TN 37203

Roger Whittaker
P.O. Box 1655-GB
London, W8 5HZ ENGLAND

Andy Williams
2500 West Highway 76
Branson, MO 65616

Hank Williams, Jr.
Hwy. 79 East
Box 1350
Paris, TN 38242

Joe Williams
2810 West Charleston #G-72
Las Vegas, NV 89102

John Williams
333 Loring Avenue
Los Angeles, CA 90024

Paul Williams
8545 Franklin Avenue
Los Angeles, CA 90069

Vanessa Williams
P.O. Box 858
Chappaqua, NY 10514

Brian Wilson
14042 Aubrey Road
Beverly Hills, CA 90210

Carnie Wilson
13601 Ventura Blvd. #286
Sherman Oaks, CA 91423

Mary Wilson
163 Amsterdam Avenue #125
New York, NY 10023

Nancy Wilson (50's Singer)
2810 West Charleston G-72
Las Vegas, NV 89102

Nancy Wilson (Heart Lead)
202 San Vicente Blvd., #4
Santa Monica, CA 90402

Wilson Phillips
1290 Avenue of the Americas #4200
New York, NY 10104

Steve Winwood
9200 Sunset Blvd., PH 15
Los Angeles, CA 90069

Bobby Womack
1048 Tatnall Street
Macon, GA 31201

Stevie Wonder
4616 Magnolia Blvd.
Burbank, CA 91505

Wynonna
325 Bridge Street
Franklin, TN 37064

Y _____ Y

"Weird" Al Yankovic
923 Westmount Drive
Los Angeles, CA 90069

Yanni
509 Hartnell Street
Monterey, CA 93940

Glen Yarborough
P.O. Box 158
Malibu, CA 90265

Trisha Yearwood
4636-316 Lebanon Pike
Nashville, TN 37076

Yellowjackets
9220 Sunset Blvd. #320
Los Angeles, CA 90069

Dwight Yoakum
1250-6th Street #401
Santa Monica, CA 90401

Jesse Colin Young
P.O. Box 31
Lancaster, NG 03584

Neil Young
8501 Wilshire Blvd., #220
Beverly Hills, CA 90211

Z _____ Z

Dweezil Zappa
P.O. Box 5265
North Hollywood, CA 91616

Moon Zappa
P.O. Box 5265
North Hollywood, CA 91616

Pinchas Zuckerman
711 West End Avenue #5K-N
New York, NY 10025

ZZ Top
P.O. Box 19744
Houston, TX 77024

Sports

They're Not A Star Until
They're A Star In Star Guide™

A _____ A

Henry "Hank" Aaron
1611 Adams Drive S.W.
Atlanta, GA 30311

Kareem Abdul-Jabbar
1436 Summitridge Drive
Beverly Hills, CA 90210

Akeem Abdul-Olajuwon
10 Greenway Plaza East
Houston, TX 77046

Andre Agassi
8921 Andre Drive
Las Vegas, NV 89113

Troy Aikman
P.O. Box 630227
Irving, TX 75063

Danny Ainge
2910 N. Central
Phoenix, AZ 85012

Amy Alcott
1411 - 5th Street #306
Santa Monica, CA 90401

Doyle Alexander
5416 Hunter Park Court
Arlington, TX 76017

Muhammad Ali
P.O. Box 187
Berrien Springs, MI 49103

Marcus Allen
433 Ward Parkway #29
Kansas City, MO 64112

Roberto Alomar
Urbana Monserrate B-56, Box 367
Salinas, PR 00751

George "Sparky" Anderson
P.O. Box 6415
Thousand Oaks, CA 91359

Mario Andretti
53 Victory Lane
Nazareth, PA 18064

Michael Andretti
3310 Airport Road
Allentown, PA 18103

Rocky Aoki
8685 NW 53rd Terrace
Miami, FL 33155

Luis Aparicio
P.O. Box 590
Cooperstown, NY 13325

Red Auerbach
780 Boylston Street
Boston, MA 02199

Paul Azinger
7847 Chick Evans Place
Sarasota, FL 34240

B   B

Tai Babilonia
13889 Valley Vista Blvd.
Sherman Oaks, CA 91423

Donovan Bailey
625 Hales Chapel Road
Gray, TN 37615

Oksana Baiul
P.O. Box 719
Simsbury, CT 06070

Ernie Banks
613 West Serano Drive
Gilbert, AZ 85233

Sir Roger Bannister
21 Bardwell Road
Oxford OX2 6SV ENGLAND

Charles Barkley
10 Greenway Plaza East
Houston, TX 77046

Don Baylor
56325 Riviera
La Quinta, CA 92253

Boris Becker
Nusslocher Strasst 51
D-69181, Leimen, GERMANY

George Bell
324 West 35th Street
Chicago, IL 60616

Albert Belle
921 Katey Rose Lane
Euclid, OH 44143

Johnny Bench
324 Bishopsbridge Drive
Cincinnati, OH 45255

Yogi Berra
P.O. Box 462
Caldwell, NJ 07006

Gary Bettenhausen
2550 Tree Farm Road
Martinsville, IN 46151

Tony Bettenhausen
109B Gasoline Alley
Speedway, IN 46222

Jerome Bettis
300 Stadium Circle
Pittsburgh, PA 15212

Craig Biggio
P.O. Box 288
Houston, TX 77001

Matt Biondi
1404 Rimer Drive
Moraga, CA 94556

Larry Bird
RR #1-Box 77A
West Baden Springs, IN 47469

Bonnie Blair
306 White Pine Road
Delafield, WI 53018

George Blanda
P.O. Box 1153
La Quinta, CA 92253

Drew Bledsoe
Sullivan Stadium-Route 1
Foxboro, MA 02035

Rocky Bleier
705 Ivy Street #2
Pittsburgh, PA 15232

Vida Blue
P.O. Box 1449
Pleasanton, CA 94566

Nicole Bobek
20 First Street
Colorado Springs, CO 80906

Wade Boggs
6006 Windham Place
Tampa, FL 33647

Brian Boitano
101 First Street #370
Los Altos, CA 94022

Barry Bonds
9595 Wilshire Blvd., #711
Beverly Hills, CA 90212

Bobby Bonilla
390 Round Hill Road
Greenwich, CT 06831

Bjorn Borg
One Erieview Plaza #1300
Cleveland, OH 44114

Riddick Bowe
1025 Vermnot Ave. NW#1025
Washington, DC 20005

Christopher Bowman
5653 Kester Avenue
Van Nuys, CA 91405

Terry Bradshaw
1925 North Pearson Lane
Roanoke, TX 76262

George Brett
P.O. Box 419969
Kansas City, MO 64141

Lou Brock
P.O. Box 28398
St. Louis, MO 63146

Jim Brown
1851 Sunset Plaza Drive
Los Angeles, CA 90069

Bill Buckner
2425 West Victory Blvd.
Meridian, ID 83642

Leroy Burrell
1801 Ocean Park Blvd. #112
Santa Monica, CA 90405

Dick Butkus
3930 Villa Costera
Malibu, CA 90265

C   C

Hector "Macho" Camacho
4751 Yaradarm Lane
Boynton Beach, FL 33436

Bert Campaneris
P.O. Box 5096
Scottsdale, AZ 85261

Earl Campbell
P.O. Box 909
Austin, TX 78767

Jose Canseco
3025 Meadow Lane
Ft. Lauderdale, FL 33331

John Cappelletti
28791 Brant Lane
Laguna Niguel, CA 92677

Jennifer Capriati
5435 Blue Heron Lane
Wesley Chapel, FL 33543

Rod Carew
5144 E. Crescent Drive
Anaheim, CA 92807

Steve Carlton
555 South Camino Del Rio #B2
Durango, CO 81301

Peter & Kitty Carruthers
22 E. 71st Street
New York, NY 10021

Billy Casper
P.O. Box 210010
Chula Vista, CA 91921

Tracy Caulkins
511 Oman Street
Nashville, TN 37203

Steve Cauthen
Cauthen Ranch
Boone County
Walton, KY 41094

Orlando Cepeda
331 Brazelton Court
Suison City, CA 94505

Rick Cerrone
63 Eisenhower
Cresskill, NJ 07626

Ron Cey
22714 Creole Road
Woodland Hills, CA 91364

Wilt Chamberlain
11111 Santa Monica Blvd., #1000
Los Angeles, CA 90025

Michael Chang
2657 Windmill Parkway #348
Henderson, NV 89014

Julio Ceasar Chavez
539 Telegraph Canyon Rd. #253
Chula Vista, CA 91910

Roger Clemens
11535 Quail Hollow
Houston, TX 77024

Sebastian Coe
Starsgood, High Barn Road
Effingham
Surrey KT24 SPW ENGLAND

Paul Coffey
633 Hawthorne Street
Birmingham, MI 48009

Nadia Comaneci
4421 Hidden Hills Road
Norman, OK 73072

Jimmy Connors
200 S. Refugio Road
Santa Ynez, CA 93460

Gerry Cooney
22501 Linden Blvd.
Jamaica, NY 11411

Bob Costas
c/o NBC Sports
30 Rockefeller Plaza
New York, NY 10112

Fred Couples
5609 Cradlerock Circle
Plano, TX 75093

Jim Courier
1 Erieview Plaza #1300
Cleveland, OH 44114

Robin Cousins
2887 Hollyridge Drive
Los Angeles, CA 90068

Bob Cousy
427 Salisbury Street
Worcester, MA 01609

Bobby Cox
P.O. Box 4064
Atlanta, GA 30302

Ben Crenshaw
2905 San Gabriel #213
Austin, TX 78703

Denny Crumm
23015 Third Street
Louisville, KY 40292

Randall Cunningham
5020 Spanish Heights Drive
Las Vegas, NV 89118

Larry Czonka
37256 Hunter Camp Road
Lisbon, OH 44432

D _____ D

Tim Daggett
1750 East Boulder Street
Colorado Springs, CO 80909

John Daly
P.O. Box 109601
Palm Beach Garden, FL 33418

Ron Darling
19 Woodland Street
Millbury, MA 01527

Al Davis
1220 Harbor Bay Parkway
Almeda, CA 94502

Dominique Dawes
P.O. Box 8400
Silver Spring, MD 20907

Oscar De La Hoya
2401 South Atlantic Blvd.
Monterey Park, CA 91754

Mary Decker (Slaney)
2923 Flintlock Street
Eugene, OR 97401

Bucky Dent
2606 Varandah Lane #816
Arlington, TX 76006

Donna Devarona
77 West 66th Street
New York, NY 10023

Gail Devers
20214 Leadwell
Canoga Park, CA 91304

Rob Dibble
54 Summitt Farms Road
Southington, CT 06489

Dan Dierdorf
13302 Buckland Hall Road
St. Louis, MO 63131

Joe DiMaggio
3230 Stirling Road
Hollywood, FL 33021

Mike Ditka
29 English Turn Drive
New Orleans, LA 70131

Terry Donohue
11918 Laurelwood
Studio City, CA 91604

Vince Dooley
P.O. Box 1472
Athens, GA 30603

Tony Dorsett
6005 Kettering Court
Dallas, TX 75248

James "Buster" Douglas
465 Waterbury Court #A
Gahanna, OH 43230

Clyde Drexler
University of Houston Basketball
Houston, TX 77277

Joe Dumars
c/o The Palace
Auburn Hills, MI 48057

Angelo Dundee
450 North Park Road #800
Hollywood, FL 33021

Lenny Dykstra
236 Chester Road
Devon, PA 19333

E   E

Dale Earnhardt
Rt. 10, Box 595-B
Mooresville, NC 28115

Dennis Eckersley
39 Plympton Road
Sudburg, MA 01776

Stefan Edberg
Spinnaregaten 6
S-59352, Vastervik, SWEDEN

Lee Elder
4130 Palm Aire Dr. W. #302B
Pompano Beach, FL 33069

Sean Elliott
P.O. Box 530
San Antonio, TX 78292

Ernie Els
P.O. Box 2255
Parklands 2121 SOUTH AFRICA

John Elway
10030 East Arapahoe Road
Englewood, CO 80112

Dick Enberg
Box 710
Rancho Santa Fe, CA 92067

Julius Erving
P.O. Box 8269
Cherry Hill, NJ 08002

Janet Evans
8 Barneburg
Dove Canyon, CA 92679

Chris Everett
500 N.E. 25th Street
Wilton Manors, FL 33305

Patrick Ewing
37 Summit Street
Englewood Cliffs, NJ 07632

F   F

Nick Faldo
Pier House
Strand on the Green
London W4 3NN ENGLAND

Brett Favre
3071 Gothic Court
Green Bay, WI 53213

Bob Feller
P.O. Box 170
Novelty, OH 44072

Mark Fidrych
260 West Street
Northboro, MA 01532

Rollie Fingers
4894 Eastcliff Court
San Diego, CA 92130

Doug Flutie
22 Robin Hood Road
Natick, MA 01760

Carlton Fisk
16612 Catawba Road
Lockport, IL 60441

Whitey Ford
38 Schoolhouse Lane
Lake Success, NY 11020

Christian Fittipaldi
282 Alphaville Barueri 064500
Sao Paulo BRAZIL

George Foreman
7639 Pine Oak Drive
Humble, TX 77397

Emerson Fittipaldi
950 S. Miami Avenue
Miami, FL 33130

A.J. Foyt
6415 Toledo
Houston, TX 77008

Peggy Fleming
1122 S. Robertson Blvd., #15
Los Angeles, CA 90035

Joe Frazier
2917 N. Broad Street
Philadelphia, PA 19132

Raymond Floyd
P.O. Box 545957
Surfside, FL 33154

Walt Frazier
400 Central Park West #7W
New York, NY 10025

G   G

Roman Gabriel
16817 McKee Road
Charlotte, NC 28278

Zina Garrison
P.O. Box 272305
Houston, TX 77277

Joe Garagiola
6221 East Huntress Drive
Paradise Valley, AZ 85253

Steve Garvey
11718 Barrington Court #6
Los Angeles, CA 90049

Randy Gardner
4640 Glencove Avenue #6
Marina Del Rey, CA 90291

Mark Gastineau
9090 North 96th Place
Scottsdale, AZ 85258

Willie Gault
33-26th Place
Venice, CA 90291

Althea Gibson (Darbeu)
275 Prospect Street #768
East Orange, NJ 07017

Bob Gibson
215 Bellevue Road South
Belleview, NE 68005

Kirk Gibson
15135 Charlevois Street
Grosse Pointe, MI 48230

Frank Gifford
625 Madison Avenue #1200
New York, NY 10022

Tom Glavine
1 CNN Center
South Tower #405
Atlanta, GA 30303

Dwight Gooden
6700-30th Street South
St. Petersburg, FL 33712

Juan Gonzalez
P.O. Box 90111
Arlington, TX 76004

Ekaterina Gordeeva
1375 Hopmeadow Street
Simsbury, CT 06070

Jeff Gordon
5325 Stowe Lane
Harrisburg, NC 28075

Curt Gowdy
33 Franklin Street
Lawrence, MA 01040

Steffi Graff
Luftschiffring 8
D-68782, Bruhl, GERMANY

Otto Graham
2216 Riviera Drive
Sarasota, FL 34232

Horace Grant
One Magic Place
Orlando, FL 32801

Dennis Green
9520 Viking Drive
Eden Prairie, MN 55344

"Mean" Joe Greene
2121 George Halas Drive NW
Canton, OH 44708

Bob Greise
3250 Mary Street
Miami, FL 33133

Wayne Gretzky
9100 Wilshire Blvd., #1000W
Beverly Hills, CA 90212

Rosey Grier
P.O. Box "A"
Santa Ana, CA 92711

Ken Griffey, Jr.
P.O. Box 4100
Seattle, WA 98104

Ken Griffey, Sr.
8216 Princeton Glendale Rd. #103
Westchester, OH 45069

Archie Griffin
4965 St. Andrews Drive
Westerville, OH 43082

Florence Griffith-Joyner
27758 Santa Margarita #38
Mission Viejo, CA 92691

Lou Groza
287 Parkway Drive
Berea, OH 44017

Pedro Guerrero
435 S. Lafayette Park Place #308
Los Angeles, CA 90057

Ron Guidry
P.O. Box 278
Scott, LA 70583

Greg Gumbel
347 W. 57th Street
New York, NY 10019

Tony Gwynn
15643 Boulder Ridge Lane
Poway, CA 92064

H   H

Marvin Hagler
75 Presidential Drive #4
Quincy, MA 02169

Dorothy Hamill
75490 Fairway Drive
Indian Wells, CA 92210

Scott Hamilton
4242 Van Nuys Blvd.
Sherman Oaks, CA 91403

Jim Harbaugh
100 South Capitol Avenue
Indianapolis, IN 46225

Anfernee Hardaway
One Magic Place
Orlando, FL 32801

Tonya Harding
121 Morrison Street SW #1100
Portland, OR 97204

Franco Harris
200 Chauser Court South
Sewickley, PA 15143

John Havlicek
24 Beech Road
Weston, CT 02193

Bob Hayes
13901 Preston Valley Place
Dallas, TX 75240

Elvin Hayes
252 Piney Point Road
Houston, TX 77024

Tommy Hearns
3645 Pama Lane
Las Vegas, NV 89120

Eric Heiden
82 Sandburg Drive
Sacramento, CA 95819

Rickey Henderson
10561 Englewood Drive
Oakland, CA 94621

Keith Hernandez
255 East 49th Street #28-D
New York, NY 10017

Orel Hershiser
1638 Via Tuscany
Winter Park, FL 32789

Whitey Herzog
9426 Sappington Estates Drive
St. Louis, MO 63127

Virgil Hill
117 Santa Gertrudis
Bismarck, ND 58501

Martina Hingus
Seidenbbaum CH-9477
Trubbach SWITZERLAND

Hulk Hogan
130 Willadel Drive
Belleair, FL 34616

Larry Holmes
91 Larry Holmes Dr. #101
Easton, PA 18042

Lou Holtz
P.O. Box 518
Notre Dame, IN 46556

Evander Holyfield
794 Highway 279
Fairburn, GA 30213

Rick Honeycutt
207 Forrest Road
Fort Oglethorpe, GA 30742

Burt Hooten
3619 Grandby Court
San Antonio, TX 78217

Paul Hornung
5800 Creighton Hill Road
Louisville, KY 40207

Willie Horton
15124 Warwick Street
Detroit, MI 48223

Ralph Houk
3000 Plantation Road
Winter Haven, FL 33884

Gordie Howe
6645 Peninsula Drive
Traverse City, MI 49684

Bobby Hull
1439 S. Indiana Avenue
Chicago, IL 60605

Jim 'Catfish' Hunter
RR #1, Box 895
Hertford, NC 27944

I   I

Michael Irvin
1 Cowboys Parkway
Irving, TX 78063

Hale Irwin
2801 Stonington Place
St. Louis, MO 63131

J   J

Bo Jackson
1765 Old Shell Road
Mobile, AL 36604

Gordon Johncock
1042 Becker Road
Hastings, MI 49056

Keith Jackson
c/o ABC Sports
1330 Avenue of Americas
New York, NY 10019

Ben Johnson
926 Stonehaven Avenue
New Market, Ont. L3X 1K7
CANADA

Reggie Jackson
305 Amador Avenue
Seaside, CA 93955

Ervin "Magic" Johnson
9100 Wilshire Blvd., #1060
West Tower
Beverly Hills, CA 90212

Dan Jansen
5040 S. 76th Street
Greenfield, WI 53220

Jimmy Johnson
2269 N.W. 199th Street
Miami, FL 33056

Lee Janzen
7512 Dr. Phillips Blvd. #50-906
Orlando, FL 32819

Michael Johnson
3101 Iris Avenue #215
Boulder, CO 80301

Bruce Jenner
P.O. Box 11137
Beverly Hills, CA 90213

Michael Jordan
676 N. Michigan Avenue #2940
Chicago, IL 60611

Tommy John
1585 Medina Road
Long Lake, MN 55356

Jackie Joyner-Kersee
P.O. Box 2220
Winnetka, CA 91396

K
K

Al Kaline
945 Timberlake Drive
Bloomfield Hills, MI 49013

Bela Karolyi
RR #1-Box 140
Huntsville, TX 77340

Anatoly Karpov
Luzhnetskaya 8
Moscow, 119270 RUSSIA

Alex Karras
7943 Woodrow Wilson Drive
Los Angeles, CA 90046

George Kell
P.O. Box 70
Swifton, AR 72471

Shawn Kemp
1 Center Court
Cleveland, OH 44115

Nancy Kerrigan
7 Cedar Avenue
Stoneham, MA 02180

Jason Kidd
201 East Jefferson Street
Phoenix, AZ 85004

Harmon Killebrew
P.O. Box 14550
Scottsdale, AZ 85267

Jeane-Claude Killey
13 Chemin Bellefontaine
1223 Cologny GE SWITZERLAND

Billie Jean King
445 North Wells #404
Chicago, IL 60610

Don King
871 West Oakland Blvd.
Oakland Park, FL 33311

Tom Kite
5999 Long Champ Court
Austin, TX 78746

Franz Klammer
Mooswald 22
A-9712, Fresach, AUSTRIA

Evel Knievel
160 E. Flamingo Road
Las Vegas, NV 89109

Bobby Knight
Indiana University Basketball
Bloomington, IN 47405

Olga Korbut
4705 Masters Ct.
Duluth, MN 30136

Bernie Kosar
6969 Ron Park Place
Youngstown, OH 44512

Sandy Koufax
100 North Broadway #2100
St. Louis, MO 63102

Jack Kramer
231 N. Glenroy Place
Los Angeles, CA 90049

Mike Krzyzewski
Duke University Basketball
Durham, NC 27706

Toni Kukoc
1901 West Madison Street
Chicago, IL 60612

Mitch Kupchak
156 North Gunston Drive
Los Angeles, CA 90049

Michelle Kwan
44450 Pinetree Drive #103
Plymouth, MI 48071

L   L

Jack LaLanne
P.O. Box 1023
San Luis Obispo, CA 93406

Donny Lalonde
2554 Lincoln Blvd., #729
Venice, CA 90291

Jack Lambert
222 Highland Drive
Carmel, CA 93921

Jake LaMotta
235 Beacon Drive
Phoenixville, PA 19460

Jim Lampley
3347 Tareco Drive
Los Angeles, CA 90068

Tom Landry
5336 Rock Cliff Place
Dallas, TX 75209

Bernhard Langer
1120 S.W. 21st Lane
Boca Raton, FL 33486

Tommy LaSorda
1473 W. Maxzim Avenue
Fullerton, CA 92633

Buddy Lazier
8135 W. Crawfordsville
Indianapolis, IN 46224

Mario Lemieux
630 Academy Street
Sewickley, PA 15143

Bob Lemon
95 Fairway Lakes
Myrtle Beach, SC 29577

Meadowlark Lemon
13610 N. Scottsdale Road #1026
Scottsdale, AZ 85254

Greg Lemond
5250 Nell Road #101
Reno, NV 89502

Ivan Lendl
400 - 5 1/2 Mile Road
Goshen, CT 05766

Sugar Ray Leonard
4401 East West Hwy., #303
Bethesda, MD 20914

Carl Lewis
P.O. Box 571990
Houston, TX 77257

Lenno Lewis
811 Totowa Road #100
Totowa, NJ 07512

Eric Lindros
1 Pattison Place
Philadelphia, PA 19148

Tara Lipinski
888 Denison Court
Bloomfield Hills, MI 48302

Howie Long
514 South Juanita Avenue
Redondo Beach, CA 90277

Nancy Lopez
2308 Tara Drive
Albany, GA 31707

Ronnie Lott
11342 Canyon View Circle
Cupertino, CA 95014

Greg Louganis
P.O. Box 4130
Malibu, CA 90264

Jerry Lucas
P.O. Box 728
Templeton, CA 93465

Johnny Lujack
6321 Crow Valley Drive
Bettendorf, IA 52722

Greg Luzinski
620 Jackson Road
Medford, NJ 08055

M   M

John Madden
5955 Corondao Blvd.
Pleasanton, CA 94588

Bill Madlock
18 Meeting House Lane
Shelton, CT 06484

Karl Malone
301 West South Temple
Salt Lake City, UT 84101

Moses Malone
1001 North 4th Street
Milwaukee, WI 53203

Ray "Boom Boom" Mancini
12524 Indianapolis Street
Los Angeles, CA 90066

Danny Manning
1 CNN Center #405
Atlanta, GA 30303

Nigel Mansell
Station Road Box 1
Ballasalle
Isle of Man ENGLAND

Diego Maradona
Brandsen 805
1161 Capital Federal ARGENTINA

Jaun Marichal
9458 NW 54 Doral Circle Lane
Miami, FL 33128

Dan Marino
3415 Stallion Lane
Ft. Lauderdale, FL 33331

Buster Mathis Jr.
4409 Carol SW
Wyoming, MI 49509

Don Mattingly
RR #5, Box 74
Evansville, IN 47711

Gene Mauch
71 Princeton
Rancho Mirage, CA 92270

Willie Mays
P.O. Box 2410
Menlo Park, CA 94026

Tim McCarver
1518 Youngford Road
Gladwnne, PA 19035

John McEnroe
23712 Malibu Colony
Malibu, CA 90265

Tug McGraw
2595 Wallingford Road
San Marino, CA 91108

Mark McGwire
1704 Alamo Plaza #322
Alamo, CA 94507

Jim McKay
2805 Sheppard Road
Monkton, MD 21111

Denny McLain
11994 Hyne Road
Brighton, MI 48116

Steve McNair
335 South Hollywood
Memphis, TN 38104

Rick Mears
204 Spyglass Lane
Jupiter, FL 33477

Don Meredith
P.O. Box 597
Santa Fe, NM 87504

Al Michaels
47 W. 66th Street
New York, NY 10023

Cheryl Miller
6767 Forest Lawn Drive #115
Los Angeles, CA 90068

Johnny Miller
P.O. Box 2260
Napa, CA 94558

Reggie Miller
11116 Catamaran Court
Indianapolis, IN 46236

Shannon Miller
P.O. Box 5103
Edmond, OK 73083

Rick Mirer
11220 NE 53rd Street
Kirkland, WA 98033

Larry Mize
106 Greystone Court
Columbus, GA 31904

Rick Monday
149 42nd Avenue
San Mateo, CA 94403

Earl Monroe
535 Boulevard
Kenilworth, NJ 07033

Joe Montana
10415 Sarah Street
Toluca Lake, CA 91602

Warren Moon
1 Lakeside Estate Drive
Missouri City, TX 77459

Archie Moore
145 Hugenot Street
New Rochelle, NY 10301

Joe Morgan
3239 Danvill Blvd., #A
Alamo, CA 94507

Alonzo Morning
701 Areana Blvd.
Miami, FL 33136

Edwin Moses
P.O. Box 120
Indianapolis, IN 46206

Manny Mota
3926 Los Olivos Lane
La Crescenta, CA 91214

Shirley Muldowney
79559 North Avenue
Armada, MI 48005

Bobby Murcer
P.O. Box 75089
Oklahoma City, OK 73147

Brent Musburger
47 West 66th Street
New York, NY 10023

Stan Musial
1655 Des Peres Road #125
St. Louis, MO 63131

Dikembe Mutombo
1 CNN Center #405
Atlanta, GA 30303

N   N

Joe Namath
7 Bay Harbor Road
Tequesta, FL 33469

Ille Nastase
Calea Plevnei 14
Bucharest HUNGARY

Martina Navratilova
1266 E. Main Street #44
Stamford, CT 06902

Byron Nelson
Rt.3, Box 5 Litsey Road
Roanoke, TX 76262

Bobby Nichols
8681 Glenlyon Ct.
Ft. Meyers, FL 33912

Jack Nicklaus
11760 U.S. Highway 1 #6
N. Palm Beach, FL 33408

Joe Niekro
2707 Fairway Drive South
Plant City, FL 33567

Phil Niekro
6382 Nichols Road
Flowery Branch, GA 30542

Yannick Noah
20 rue Billancourt
91200 Bolougne FRANCE

Chuck Noll
201 Grang Street
Sewickley, PA 15143

Greg Norman
501 North Aia Ste.
Jupiter, FL 33477

Ken Norton
20451 Puerto Vallerta Drive
Laguna Niguel, CA 92677

O   O

Dan O'Brien
P.O. Box 9344
Moscow, ID 83843

Hakeem Olajuwon
10 Greenway Plaza East
Houston, TX 77046

Shaquille O'Neal
3110 Main Street #225
Santa Monica, CA 90405

Bobby Orr
300 Boylston Street #605
Boston, MA 02116

P   P

Billy Packer
c/o CBS Sports
51 W. 52nd Street
New York, NY 10019

Arnold Palmer
100 Avenue of Champions
Palm Beach Gardens, FL 33418

Jim Palmer
P.O. Box 590
Cooperstown, NY 13326

Jack Pardee
P.O. Box 272
Grause, TX 77857

Dave Parker
7864 Ridge Road
Cincinnati, OH 45237

Ara Parseghien
240 Seaview Court PH A
Marco, FL 33937

Joe Paterno
830 McKee Street
State College, PA 16803

Floyd Patterson
Springtown Road
Box 336
New Paltz, NY 12561

Corey Paven
2515 McKinney #930, Box 10
Dallas, TX 75201

Walter Payton
13400 South Budler Road
Plainfield, IL 60544

Rodney Peete
10683 Santa Monica Blvd.
Los Angeles, CA 90025

Pele
Praca dos Tres Poderes
palacio de Planalto BR
70150900 Brasilia DF BRAZIL

Roger Penske
13400 Outer Drive West
Detroit, MI 48239

Joe Pepitone
32 Lois Lane
Farmingdale, NY 11735

Gaylord Perry
P.O. Box 1958
Kill Devil Hills, NC 27948

Kyle Petty
135 Longfield Drive
Mooresville, NC 28115

Richard Petty
311 Branson Mill Rd., Box 86
Randleman, NC 27317

Mary Pierce
5500 - 34th Street West
Bradenton, FL 34210

Lou Piniella
1005 Taray De Avila
Tampa, FL 33613

Vada Pinson
710-31st Street
Oakland, CA 94609

Scottie Pippen
c/o General Delivery
Highland Park, IL 60035

R

Bobby Rahal
P.O. Box 39
Hillard, OH 43026

Willie Randolph
648 Juniper Place
Franklin Lakes, NJ 07417

Ahmad Rashad
30 Rockefeller Plaza #1411
New York, NY 10020

Pee Wee Reese
1400 Willow Avenue
Louiseville, KY 40204

Mary Lou Retton
44450 Pinetree Drive #103
Plymouth MI 48170

Dusty Rhodes
8577A Boca Glades Blvd. West
Boca Raton, FL 33434

Gary Player
3930 RCA Blvd., #3001
Palm Beach Gardens, FL 33410

Jim Plunkett
51 Kilroy Way
Atherton, CA 94025

Nick Price
300 South Beach Road
Hobe Sound, FL 33455

R

Jerry Rice
2 Brittany Meadows
Atherton, CA 94025

Jim Rice
RR #8
Anderson, SC 29621

Bobby Richardson
P.O. Box 2000
Lynchburg, VA 24506

Dot Richarson
USC Medical Center
1200 N. State Street #GH-3900
Los Angeles, CA 90033

Cathy Rigby
110 E. Wilshire #200
Fullerton, CA 92632

Jim Riggleman
1060 West Addison Street
Chicago, IL 60613

Pat Riley
180 Arvida Parkway
Miami, FL 33156

Cal Ripken, Jr.
2330 W. Juppa Road #333
Lutherville, MD 21093

Cal Ripken, Sr.
410 Clover Street
Aberdeen, MD 21001

Mickey Rivers
350 NW 48th Street
Miami, FL 33127

Phil Rizzuto
912 Westminster Avenue
Hillside, NJ 07205

Oscar Robertson
621 Tuschulum Avenue
Cincinnati, OH 45226

Brooks Robinson
36 S. Charles Street #2000
Baltimore, MD 21201

David Robinson
P.O. Box 530
San Antonio, TX 78292

Frank Robinson
15557 Aqua Verde Drive
Los Angeles, CA 90024

Glen Robinson
1001 North Fourth Street
Milwaukee, WI 53203

Dennis Rodman
4809 Seashore Drive
Newport Beach, CA 92663

Alex Rodriquez
P.O. Box 4100
Seattle, WA 98104

Chi Chi Rodriguez
P.O. Box 5118
Akron, OH 44334

Ivan Rodriguez
P.O. Box 90111
Arlington, TX 76004

Bill Rogers
353 The Marketplace
Fanuil Hall
Boston, MA 02109

Jaelen Rose
300 East Marketplace Street
Indianapolis, IN 46204

Pete Rose
8144 Glades Road
Boca Raton, FL 33434

Ken Rosewall
111 Pentacost Avenue
Turramurra, NSW
2074, AUSTRALIA

Kyle Rote
24700 Deepwater Point Drive #14
St. Michaels, MD 21663

Kyle Rote Jr.
6075 Poplar Avenue #920
Memphis, TN 38119

Darrell Royal
10507 La Costa Drive
Austin, TX 78747

Pete Rozelle
P.O. Box 9686
Rancho Santa Fe, CA 92067

Johnny Rutherford
4919 Black Oak Lane
Ft. Worth, TX 76114

Nolan Ryan
200 West South Street #B
Alvin, TX 77511

S

S

Gabriela Sabatini
Ap. Int 14 Suc. 27
1427 Buenos Aires, ARGENTINA

Brett Saberhagen
5535 Amber Circle
Calabasas, CA 91302

Pete Sampras
6352 MacLaurin Drive
Tampa, FL 33647

Barry Sanders
1200 Featherstone Road
Pontiac, MI 48057

Deion Sanders
10250 Meadow Crest Lane
Alpharetta, GA 30083

Summer Sanders
730 Sunrise Avenue
Roseville, CA 95661

Ron Santo
1721 Meadow Lane
Bannockburn, IL 60015

Randy "Macho Man" Savage
13300 Indian Rocks Road #304
Largo, FL 33774

Gale Sayers
624 Buck Road
Northbrook, IL 60062

Bo Schembechler
1904 Boulder Drive
Ann Arbor, MI 48104

Mike Scioscia
444 Fargo Street
Thousand Oaks, CA 91360

Junior Seau
9449 Friars Road
San Diego, CA 92108

Tom Seaver
Larkspur Lane
Greenwich, CT 06830

Monica Seles
7751 Beeridge Road
Sarasota, FL 34241

Bud Selig
c/o County Coliseum
Milwaukee, WI 53214

Gary Sheffield
2267 NW 199th Street
Miami, FL 33056

Art Shell
2318 Walker Drive
Lawrenceville, GA 30043

Bill Shoemaker
2553 Fairfield Place
San Marino, CA 91108

Pam Shriver
133 - 1st Street NE
St. Petersburg, FL 33701

Don Shula
16 Indian Creek Island
Miami Lakes, FL 33154

Rubin Sierra
Ed 25 #2501 Jardines Selles
Rio Piedras, PR 00924

Phil Simms
252 W. 71st Street
New York, NY 10023

O.J. Simpson
11661 San Vicente Blvd., #632
Los Angeles, CA 90049

Bruce Smith
One Bill Drive
Orchard Park, NY 14127

Emmitt Smith
1 Cowboys Parkway
Irving, TX 78063

J.C. Snead
1751 Pinnacle Drive #1500
McLean, VA 22102

Sam Snead
P.O. Box 839
Hot Springs, VA 24445

Tom Sneva
3301 E. Valley Vista Lane
Paradise Valley, AZ 85253

Annika Sorenstam
1000 Avenue of the Champions
Palm Beach Gardens, FL 33418

Warren Spahn
Route #2
Hartshorne, OK 74547

Boris Spassky
Skatertny Pereulok 5
Moscow RUSSIA

Leon Spinks
P.O. Box 88771
Carol Stream IL 60188

Michael Spinks
250 W. 57th Street
New York, NY 10107

Mark Spitz
383 Dalehurst
Los Angeles, CA 90077

Steve Spurrier
12115 NW 1st Lane
Gainesville, FL 32907

Ken Stabler
Rt. Box, General Delivery
Orange Beach, AL 36561

Eddie Stanky
2100 Spring Hill Road
Mobile, AL 36607

Willie Stargell
813 Tarpon Drive
Wilmington, NC 28409

Bart Starr
2065 Royal Fern Lane
Birmingham, AL 35244

Roger Staubach
7912 Edelweiss Circle
Dallas, TX 75240

George Steinbrenner
P.O. Box 25077
Tampa, FL 33622

Jan Stephenson
1231 Garden Street #204
Titusville, FL 32769

David Stern
645 - 5th Avenue
New York, NY 10022

Jackie Stewart
24 Rte. de Divonne
1260, Nyon, SWITZERLAND

Payne Stewart
390 N. Orange Avenue #2600
Orlando, FL 32801

John Stockton
301 West South Temple
Salt Lake City, UT 84101

Hank Stram
194 Belle Terre Blvd.
Covington, LA 70483

Curtis Strange
137 Thomas Dale
Williamsburg, VA 23185

Darryl Strawberry
P.O. Box 17868
Encino, CA 91316

Kerri Strug
2801 North Camino Princlpal
Tuscon, AZ 85715

Danny Sullivan
414 East Cooper Street #201
Aspen, CO 81611

Don Sutton
1145 Mountain Ivy Drive
Roswell, GA 30075

Lynn Swann
600 Grant Street #4800
Pittsburgh, PA 15219

Sheryl Swoopes
1751 Pinnacle Drive #1500
McLean, VA 22102

T _____ **T**

Paul Tagliabue
410 Park Avenue
New York, NY 10022

Roscoe Tanner
1109 Gnome Trail
Lookout Mountain, TN 37350

Fran Tarkington
1431 Garmon Ferry Road NW
Atlanta, GA 30327

Lawrence Taylor
122 Canterbury Lane
Williamsburg, VA 23188

Ernie Terrell
11136 South Parnell
Chicago, IL 60628

Vinny Testaverde
936 Crenshaw Lake Road
Lutz, FL 33549

Joe Theisman
5912 Leesburg Pike
Falls Church, VA 22041

Debi Thomas
22 E. 71st Street
New York, NY 10021

Frank Thomas
c/o Comiskey Park
Chicago, IL 60616

Isaiah Thomas
710 Lone Pine Road
Bloomfield, MI 48304

Thurman Thomas
One Bill Drive
Orchard Park, NY 14127

John Thompson
Georgetown University Basketball
Washington, DC 20057

Y.A. Tittle
P.O. Box 571
Lebanon, IN 46052

Alberto Tomba
I-40068 Castel de Britti
ITALY

Mike Tomczak
c/o Three River Stadium
Pittsburgh, PA 15212

James Toney
6305 Wellesley
West Bloomfield, MI 48322

Joe Torre
c/o Yankee Stadium
Bronx, NY 10451

Gwen Torrence
P.O. Box 361965
Decatur, GA 30036

Torville & Dean
Box 16, Beeston
Nottingham NG9 ENGLAND

Tony Trabert
115 Knotty Pine Trail
Ponte Vedra, FL 32082

Lee Trevino
1901 W. 47th Place #200
Westwood, KS 6205

Mike Tyson
501 Fairway Drive
Deerfield Beach, FL 33441

U   U

Bob Uecker
201 South 46th Street
Milwaukee, WI 53214

Johnny Unitas
5607 Patterson Road
Baldwin, MD 21013

Al Unser
7625 Central N.W.
Albuquerque, NM 87105

Bobby Unser
7700 Central S.W.
Albuquerque, NM 87105

Bobby Unser Jr.
P.O. Box 25047
Albuquerque, NM 87125

Gene Upshaw
1102 Pepper Tree Drive
Great Falls, VA 22066

V   V

Fernando Valenzuela
3004 N. Beachwood Drive
Los Angeles, CA 90027

Mo Vaugh
c/o Fenway Park
Boston, MA 62215

Ken Venturi
P.O. Box 5118
Akron, OH 44334

Dick Vermeil
51 W. 52nd Street
New York, NY 10019

Guillermo Vilas
Avenue Foch 86
Paris, FRANCE

Frank Viola
844 Sweetwater Island Circle
Longwood, FL 32779

W   W

Virginia Wade
Sharstead Court
Sittingbourne, Kent, ENGLAND

Lanny Wadkins
6002 Kettering Court
Dallas, TX 75248

Greta Waitz
Birgitte Hammers Vei 15-G
1169 Oslo NORWAY

Doak Walker
P.O. Box 77329
Steamboat Springs, CO 80477

Bill Walsh
Stanford University Football
Stanford, CA 94305

Bill Walton
1010 Myrtle Way
San Diego, CA 92103

Darrell Waltrip
6780 Hudseth Road
Harrisburg, NC 28705

Malivai Washington
1101 Wilson Blvd., #1800
Arlington, VA 22209

Tom Watson
1901 West 47th Place #200
Westwood, KS 66205

Earl Weaver
501 Cypress Pt. Drive W.
Pembroke Pines, FL 33027

Chris Webber
31487 Northwestern Hwy #A
Farmington Hills, MI 48334

Tom Weiskopf
7580 East Gray Road
Scottsdale, AZ 85260

Walt Weiss
P.O. Box 4064
Atlanta, GA 30302

Jerry West
P.O. Box 10
Inglewood, CA 903006

Lou Whitaker
803 Pipe Street
Martinsville, VA 24112

Reggie White
P.O. Box 10628
Green Bay, WI 54307

Mats Wilander
Vickersvagen 2
Vaxjo, SWEDEN

Hoyt Wilhelm
3102 N. Himes Avenue
Tampa, FL 33607

Lanny Wilkens
2660 Peachtree Road NW #39F
Atlanta, GA 30305

Jamaal Wilkes
7846 West 81st Street
Playa del Rey, CA 90291

Billy Williams
586 Prince Edward Road
Glen Ellyn, IL 60137

Matt Williams
c/o Candlestick Park
San Francisco, CA 94124

Ted Williams
2448 North Essex Avenue
Hernando, FL 33441

Dave Winfield
11809 Gwynne Lane
Los Angeles, CA 90077

Katarina Witt
Lindenstr. 8
16244 Altenhof, GERMANY

Todd Woodbridge
1751 Pinnacle Drive #1500
McLean, VA 22102

John Wooden
17711 Margate St. #102
Encino, CA 91316

Tiger Woods
4281 Katella Avenue #111
Los Alamitos, CA 90720

Y   Y

Kristi Yamaguchi
3650 Montecito Drive
Fremont, CA 94536

Caleb Yarborough
9617 Dixie River Road
Charlotte, NC 28270

Carl Yastrzemski
4621 S. Ocean Blvd.
Highland Beach, FL 33431

Steve Young
261 East Broadway
Salt Lake City, UT 84111

Z   Z

Don Zimmer
10124 Yacht Club Drive
St. Petersburg, FL 33706

"Fuzzy" Zoeller
418 Deer Run Terrace
Floyd's Knobs, IN 47119

Politics

They're Not A Star Until
They're A Star In Star Guide™

A   A

Gerry Adams
51/55 Falls Road
Belfast BT 12
NORTHERN IRELAND

King Bhumibol Adulyadey
Villa Chitralada
Bangkok, THAILAND

Sen. Daniel K. Akaka (HI)
Senate Hart Bldg. #720
Washington, DC 20510

Emperor Akihoto
The Imperial Palace
Tokyo, JAPAN

President Hafez Al-Assad
Office of the President
Damascus, SYRIA

Prince Albert of Monaco
Palais De Monace
Boite Postal 518
98015 Monte Carlo, MONACO

Medeleine Albright
1318-34th Street NW
Washington, DC 20007

Ex-Gov. Lamar Alexander
1109 Owen Place N.E.
Washington, DC 20008

Idi Amin
P.O. Box 8948,
Jidda 21492 Saudi Arabia

Prince Andrew of England
Sunninghill Park
Windsor, ENGLAND

Kofi Annan
799 United Nations Plaza
New York, NY 10017

Princess Anne of England
Gatcombe Park
Gloucestershire, ENGLAND

Corazon Aquino
c/o Pius XVl Center, UN
Manila PHILIPPINES

Yassir Arafat
Gaza City, Gaza Strip
Palestine ISREAL

Rep. Bill Archer (TX)
House Longworth Bldg. #1236
Washington, DC 20515

Dennis Archer
2 Woodward Avenue
Detroit, MI 49226

Moshe Arens
49 Hagderat
Savyon, ISREAL

Oscar Arias
Apdo 8-6410-1000
San Jose COSTA RICA

B   B

Sec. Bruce Babbitt
5169 Watson Street NW
Washington, DC 20016

Ex-Sen. Howard Baker
P.O. Box 8
Huntsville, TN 37756

James Baker III
1299 Pennsylvania Avenue, NW
Washington, DC 20004

Marion Barry
161 Raleigh Street SE
Washington, DC 20032

Birch Bayh
1575 "I" Street #1025
Washington, DC 20005

Abraham Beame
1111-20th Street NW
Washington, D.C. 20575

Queen Beatrix of Holland
Kasteel Drakesteijn
Lage Vuursche, 3744 BA
HOLLAND

Griffen Bell
206 Townsend Place NW
Atlanta, GA 30727

Sen. Robert F. Bennett (UT)
Senate Dirksen Bldg., #431
Washington, D.C. 20510

P.M. Benazir Bhutto
70 Clifton Road
Karachi, Pakistan

Sen. Joseph Biden, Jr. (DL)
221 Russel, Sen. Office Bldg.
Washington, DC 20510

Sen. Jeff Bingaman (NM)
Senate Hart Building #703
Washington, DC 20510

Tony Blair
#10 Downing Street
London SW1 ENGLAND

Julian Bond
4805 Mt. Hope Drive
Baltimore, MD 20215

Rep. David Bonior (MI)
House Rayburn Building #2207
Washington, DC 20515

Boutros Boutros-Ghail
2 Avenue El Nil
Giza, Cairo EGYPT

Sen. Barbara Boxer (CA)
Senate Hart Bldg. #112
Washington, DC 20510

Bill Bradley
4 Hawthorn Avenue
Princeton, NJ 08540

Ex-Mayor Tom Bradley
3631 Mt. Vernon Drive
Los Angeles, CA 90008

James & Sarah Brady
1255 "I" Street #1100
Washington, DC 20005

Sen. John Breaux (LA)
Senate Hart Building #516
Washington, DC 20510

Justic Steven Breyer
1 - 1st Street N.E.
Washington, DC 20543

Rep. George E. Brown (CA)
2300 Rayburn, Hse. Office Bldg.
Washington, DC 20515

Sen. Hank Brown (CO)
Senate Hart Building #716
Washington, DC 20510

Ex-Gov. Jerry Brown
295 Third Street
Oakland, CA 94607

Sec. Jesse Brown
810 Vermont Avenue N.W.
Washington, DC 20420

Willie L. Brown, Jr.
401 Van Ness Avenue #336
San Francisco, CA 94102

Sen. Richard Bryan (NV)
Senate Russell Building #364
Washington, DC 20510

Zbigniew Brzezinski
1800 "K" Street NW #400
Washington, DC 20006

Patrick J. Buchanan
1017 Saville Lane North
McLean, VA 22101

Sen. Dale Bumpers (AR)
7613 Honesty Way
Bethesda, MD 20817

Jim Bunning
7410 New LaGrange Road #130
Louisville, KY 40222

Sen. Conrad Burns (MT)
Senate Dirksen Building #187
Washington, DC 20510

Barbara Bush
9 West Oak Drive
Houston, TX 77056

Ex-President George Bush
9 West Oak Drive
Houston, TX 77056

Gov. George Bush, Jr. (TX)
P.O. Box 12428
Austin, TX 78711

Gatsha Mangosuthu Buthelezi
Union Bldg
Petoria 0001 SOUTH AFRICA

Sen. Robert Byrd (WV)
311 Hart, Sen. Office Bldg.
Washington, DC 20510

C   C

Sen. Ben Campbell (CO)
456 New Jersey Avenue SE
Washington, DC 20003

Ex-PM Kim Campbell
Canadian Consulate
550 South Hope Street
Los Angeles, CA 90071

King Juan Carlos
Palace De La Carcuela
Madrid, SPAIN

Gov. Arne Carlson (MN)
130 State Capitol
St. Paul, MN 55155

Caroline, Princess of Monaco
Villa Le Clos St. Pierre Avenue
St. Martin Monte Carlo MONACO

Ex-Pres. Jimmy Carter
1 Woodland Drive
Plains, GA 31780

Rosalynn Carter
1 Woodland Drive
Plains, GA 31780

James Carville
209 Pennsylvania Avenue SE, #800
Washington, DC 20003

Dr. Fidel Castro
Palacio del Gobierno
Havana, CUBA

Sen. John H. Chafee (RI)
506 Dirksen, Sen. Office Bldg.
Washington, DC 20510

HRH Prince Charles
Highgrove House
Gloucestershire ENGLAND

Dick Cheny
500 N. Akard Street, #3600
Dallas, TX 75201

Gov. Lawton Chiles (FL)
The Capitol
Tallahassee, FL 32301

Jacques Chirac
Palais de l'Elysses
55 rue du Faubourg-St. Honore
F-75008 Paris FRANCE

Shirley Chisholm
80 Wentworth Lane
Palm Coast, FL 32137

Jean Chretien
24 Sussex Drive
Ottawa, Ontario
K1M 0MS CANADA

Warren Christopher
400 S. Hope Street #1060
Los Angeles, CA 90071

Henry Cisneros
2478 Devonport Lane
Los Angeles, CA 90077

Ex-PM Joe Clark
707 - 7th Avenue SW #1300
Calgary, Alb. T2P 3H6 CANADA

Ramsey Clark
36 E. 12th Street
New York, NY 10003

Clark Clifford
9421 Rockville Pike
Bethesda, MD 20814

President Bill Clinton
1600 Pennsylvania Avenue
Washington, DC 20505

Chelsea Clinton
Stanford University
Wilbur Hall
Palo Alto, CA 94305

Hillary Rodham Clinton
1600 Pennsylvania Avenue
Washington, DC 20505

Sen. Dan Coats (IN)
Senate Russell Bldg. #404
Washington, DC 20510

Sen. Thad Cochran (MS)
Senate Russell Building #326
Washington, DC 20510

Sec. William S. Cohen
The Pentagon,
Room 2E777 #1400
Washington, DC 20201

Rep. Cardiss Collins (IL)
2308 Rayburn, Hse. Office Bldg.
Washington, DC 20515

Sen. Kent Conrad (ND)
Senate Dirksen Building #724
Washington, DC 20510

Ex-King Constantine
4 Linnell Drive
Hampstead Way
London, NW11, ENGLAND

Rep. John Conyers (MI)
2426 Rayburn, Hse. Office Bldg.
Washington, DC 20515

Sen. Paul Coverdell (GA)
Senate Russell Building #200
Washington, DC 20510

Archibald Cox
34 Old Connecticut Path
Wayland, MA 01778

Sen. Larry Craig (ID)
Senate Hart Building #313
Washington, DC 20510

Rep. Phillip Crane (IL)
House Cannon Building #233
Washington, DC 20515

Jean Cretien
24 Sussex Drive
Ottawa, Ontario
K1M 0MS CANADA

Sec. Andrew Cuomo
Department of Housing & Urban
Development
Washington, DC 20410

Ex-Gov. Mario Cuomo
50 Sutton Place South #11-G
New York, NY 10022

D   D

Mayor Richard Daley
City Hall, 5th Floor
121 N. Lasalle Street
Chicago, IL 60602

Sec. William Daley
Department of Commerce
Washington, DC 20230

Sen. Alfonse M. D'Amato (NY)
Senate Hart Building #520
Washington, DC 20510

Ex-Sen. John C. Danforth
Rout 1, Box 91
Newburg, MO 65550

Sen. Thomas Daschle (SD)
Senate Hart Building #509
Washington, DC 20510

Ex-Sen. Dennis DeConcini
6014 Chesterbrook Road
MacLean, VA 22101

Ex-President W. F. deKlerk
Box 1692, Groenkloof
0027 Pretoria SOUTH AFRICA

Ex-Gov. George Deukmejian
555 West 5th Street
Los Angeles, CA 90013

Sen. Mike DeWine (OH)
Senate Russell Building #140
Washington, DC 20510

Rep. John Dingell (MI)
2328 Rayburn, Hse. Office Bldg.
Washington, DC 20515

David Dinkins
625 Madison Avenue
New York, NY 10022

Sen. Christopher Dodd (CT)
Senate Russell Building #444
Washington, DC 20510

Elizabeth Dole
9909 Collins Avenue
Bal Harbour, FL 33154

Ex-Sen. Robert Dole
9909 Collins Avenue
Bal Harbour, FL 33154

Sen. Pete Domenici (NM)
328 Dirksen Senate Office Bldg.
Washington, DC 20510

Ex-Rep. Robert Dornan
12387 Lewis Street #203
Garden Grove, CA 92640

Ex-Gov. Michael Dukakis
85 Perry Street
Brookline, MA 02146

Ex-Gov. Pierre duPont
Patterns
Rockland, DE 19732

E _____ E

Lawrence Eagleburger
350 Park Avenue #2600
New York, NY 10022

Ex-Sen. Thomas Eagleton
1 Mercantile Center
St. Louis, MO 63101

Gov. Jim Edgar (IL)
Office of the Governor
State House
Springfield, IL 62706

Prince Edward
Buckingham Palace
London, SW1, ENGLAND

Dr. Joycelyn Elders
800 Marshall Street
Little Rock, AR 72202

HRH Queen Elizabeth II
Buckingham Palace
London, SW1, ENGLAND

HRH Elizabeth, Queen Mother
Clarence House
London, SW1, ENGLAND

Emir of Bahrain
721 Fifth Avenue, 60th Floor
New York, NY 10022

Emir of Kuwait
Bayan Palace
Kuwait City, KUWAIT

Gov. John Engler (MI)
101 N. Capitol
Lansing, MI 48909

Rep. Anna G. Eshoo (CA)
House Cannon Building #308
Washington, DC 20515

Charles Evers
416 West County Line Road
Tougaloo, MS 39174

Myrlie Evers-Williams
4805 Mt. Hope Drive
Baltimore, MD 21215

Sen. James Exon (NE)
Senate Hart Building #528
Washington, DC 20510

F _____ F

King Fahd
Royal Palace
Riyadh, SAUDI ARABIA

Dante Fascell
6300 SW 99th Terrace
Miami, FL 33156

Sen. Russell Feingold (WI)
Senate Hart Building #SH-502
Washington, DC 20510

Sen. Dianne Feinstein (CA)
Senate Hart Building #331
Washington, DC 20510

Geraldine Ferraro
22 Deepdene Road
Forest Hills, NY 11375

Marlin Fitzwater
2001 Swan Terrace
Alexandria, VA 22307

Ex- Rep. Thomas Foley
601 West 1st Avenue #2W
Spokane, WA 99204

Betty Ford
40365 San Dune Road
Rancho Mirage, CA 92270

Ex-Pres. Gerald R. Ford
40365 San Dune Road
Rancho Mirage, CA 92270

Sen. Wendell Ford (KY)
Senate Russell Building #173A
Washington, DC 20510

Rep. Barney Frank (MA)
House Rayburn Building #2210
Washington, DC 20515

William Freeh
Federal Bureau of Investigation
9th & Pennsylvania Avenue, NW
Washington, DC 20535

G   G

Col. Mu' ammar Gaddafi
State Office/Babel Aziziya
Tripoli, LIBYA

Harvey Gantt
P.O. Box 726
Arden, NC 28704

Rep. Richard Gephart (MO)
House Longworth Building #1226
Washington, DC 20515

Rep. Newt Gingrich (GA)
House Rayburn Building #2428
Washington, DC 20515

Ruth Bader Ginsburg
700 New Hampshire Avenue NW
Washington, DC 20037

Mayor Rudolph Giuliani
City Hall
New York, NY 10007

Sen. John Glenn (OH)
1000 Urlin Avenue
Columbus, OH 43212

Ex-Chmn. Mikhail Gorbachev
49 Leningradsky Prospekt 209
Moscow RUSSIA.

V.P. Albert Gore, Jr.
34th & Massachusetts
Washington, DC 20005

Tipper Gore
34th & Massachusetts
Washington, DC 20005

Sen. Slade Gorton (WA)
Senate Hart Bldg. #730
Washington, DC 20510

Sen. Bob Graham (FL)
Senate Hart Building #524
Washington, DC 20510

Sen. Phil Gramm (TX)
Senate Russell Building #370
Washington, DC 20510

Ex- Rep. Fred Grandy
9417 Spruce Tree Circle
Bethesda, MD 20814

Sen. Charles E. Grassley (IA)
Senate Hart Bldg. #135
Washington D.C. 20510

Alan Greenspan
Federal Reserve System
20th St. & Constitution Ave. NW
Washington, DC 20551

H   H

Sen. Chuck Hager (NE)
Hart Senate Office Bldg. #528
Washington, DC 20515

Gen. Alexander Haig, Jr.
6041 Crimson Court
McLean, VA 22101

Gus Hall
235 W. 23rd Street
New York, NY 10011

Rep. Lee Hamilton (IN)
House Rayburn Building #2314
Washington, DC 20515

Sen. Tom Harkin (IA)
Senate Hart Building #531
Washington, DC 20515

Ex-Sen. Gary Hart
1999 Broadway #2236
Denver, CO 80202

King Hassan II
Royal Palace
Rabat, MOROCCO

Rep. Alcee Hastings (FL)
House Longworth Building #1039
Washington, DC 20515

Sen. Orrin G. Hatch (UT)
Senate Russell Building #131
Washington, DC 20510

Pres. Vaclav Havel
Hradecek, CZ-11908
Praha, CZECH REPUBLIC

Tom Hayden
10951 West Pico Blvd. #202
Los Angeles, CA 90064

Howell Heflin
311 E. 6th Street
Tuscumbia, AL 35674

Sen. Jesse Helms (NC)
Senate Dirken Building #403
Washington, DC 20510

Rep. Wally Herger (CA)
Rayburn House Office Bldg. #2433
Washington, DC 20515

Sec. Alexis M. Herman
Department of Labor
Washington, DC 20210

Sen. Ernest F. Hollings (SC)
Russell Senate Office Bldg. #125
Washington, DC 20510

Herbert Hoover III
200 S. Los Robles Avenue #520
Pasadena, CA 91101

Ex-Rep. Michael Huffington
3005-45th Street NW
Washington, DC 20016

Hubert H. Humphrey III
555 Park Street #310
St. Paul, MN 55103

Douglas Hurd
5 Mitford Cottage, Westwell
Burford OXON ENGLAND

Saddam Hussein
Al-Sijoud Palace
Baghdad, IRAQ

King Hussein I
Box 1055
Amman, JORDAN

Sen. Kay Bailey Hutchinson (TX)
Russell Senate Office Bldg. #283
Washington, DC 20515

Rep Henry J. Hyde (IL)
Rayburn House Office Bldg. #2110
Washington, DC 20515

J   J

Rev. Jesse Jackson
400 "T" Street NW
Washington, DC 20001

Rep. Jesse Jackson, Jr. (IL)
House Cannon Bldg. #312
Washington, D.C. 20515

Maynard Jackson
68 Mitchell
Atlanta, GA 30303

Lady Bird Johnson
LBJ Ranch
Stonewall, TX 78671

Sen. Tim Johnson (SD)
Russell Senate Office Bldg. #243
Washington, DC 20510

Vernon Jordan, Jr.
1333 New Hampshire Ave. NW #400
Washington, DC 20036

K   K

Mickey Kantor
5019 Klingle Street, NW
Washington, DC 20016

Sen. John F. Kerry (MA)
Senate Russell Building #421
Washington, DC 20510

Jack Kemp
1776 "I" Street NW #800
Washington, DC 20006

Dr. Alan Keyes
1030-15th Street NW #700
Washington, DC 20005

Sen. Dirk Kempthorne (ID)
Senate Dirksen Building #367
Washington, DC 20510

Lane Kirkland
815 - 16th Street N.W.
Washington, DC 20006

Justice Anthony Kennedy
1 - 1st Street, N.E.
Washington, DC 20543

Dr. Henry Kissinger
435 E. 52nd Street
New York, NY 10022

Rep. Joseph P. Kennedy II (MA)
House Rayburn Building #2242
Washington, DC 20515

President Tomas Klestil
Hofburg, Ballhauplatz
1010 Vienna AUSTRIA

Rep. Patrick Kennedy (RI)
House Longworth Building #1505
Washington, DC 20515

Ex-Mayor Edward I. Koch
1290 Avenue of the Americas
New York, NY 10104

Sen. Ted Kennedy (MA)
Senate Russell Building #315
Washington, DC 20510

Chancellor Helmut Kohl
Marbacher Strasse II
D-6700, Ludwigshafen
Rhein, GERMANY

Sen. Bob Kerry (NE)
Senate Hart Building #303
Washington, DC 20510

Sen. Herbert Kohl (WI)
Senate Hart Building #330
Washington, DC 20510

Mayor Teddy Kollek
22 Jaffa Road
Jerusalem, ISRAEL

Sen. Jon Kyl (AZ)
Hart Senate Office Bldg. #702
Washington, DC 20510

L   L

Ex-Gov. Richard Lamm
University of Denver
Center for Public Policy
Denver, CO 80208

Bert Lance
P.O. Box 637
Calhoun, GA 30701

Sen. Mary Landrieu (LA)
Hart Senate Office Bldg. #136
Washington, DC 20510

Rep. Tom Lantos (CA)
Rayburn House Office Bldg #2217
Washington, DC 20515

Rep. Steve Largent (OK)
Cannon House Office Building #410
Washington, DC 20515

Sen. Frank Lautenberg (NJ)
Senate Hart Building #506
Washington, DC 20510

Paul Laxalt
1455 Pennsylvania Avenue NW
Washington, D.C. 20004

Rep. Jim Leach (IA)
House Rayburn Building #2186
Washington, DC 20515

Sen. Patrick J. Leahy (VT)
Senate Russell Building #433
Washington, DC 20510

Gov. Mike Leavitt (UT)
210 State Capitol
Salt Lake City, UT 84114

Sen. Carl Levin (MI)
459 Russell, Sen. Office Bldg.
Washington, DC 20510

Rep. Jerry Lewis (CA)
House Rayburn Building #2112
Washington, DC 20515

Rep. John Lewis (GA)
House Cannon Building #229
Washington, DC 20515

Sen. Joseph I Lieberman (CT)
Senate Hart Building #316
Washington, DC 20510

Premier Li Peng
Office of the Premie
Beijing (Peking)
People Republic of China

Sen. Trent Lott (MS)
Senate Russell Building #487
Washington, DC 20510

Rep. Nita Lowey (NY)
House Rayburn Building #2421
Washington, DC 20515

Sen. Richard Lugar (IN)
Senate Hart Building #306
Washington, DC 20510

M

M

Sen. Connie Mack (FL)
Senate Hart Building #517
Washington, DC 20510

Ex. Gov. Lester Maddox
3155 Johnson Ferry NE
Marietta, GA 30062

John Major
8 Stuckley Road
Huntingdon, Cambs. ENGLAND

Charles T. Manatt
4814 Woodway Lane N.W.
Washington, DC 20016

President Nelson Mandela
51 Plain Street
Johannesburg, 2001 SOUTH AFRICA

Winnie Mandela
Orlando West, Soweto
Johannesbury SOUTH AFRICA

Imelda Marcos
Leyte Providencia Department
Tolosa, Leyte PHILIPPINES

Sen. John McCain (AZ)
Russell, Sen. Office Bldg. #241
Washington, DC 20515

Ex-Sen. Eugene J. McCarthy
271 Hawlin Road
Woodville, VA 22749

Ex-Rep. Pete McCloskey
580 Mountain Home Road
Woodside, CA 94062

Rep. Bill McCollum (FL)
House Rayburn Bldg. #2266
Washington, DC 20515

Sen. Mitch McConnell (KY)
Senate Russell Building #361A
Washington, DC 20510

Ex-Sen. George McGovern
4012 Linnean Avenue NW
Washington, DC 20008

Rep. Cynthia McKinney (GA)
House Cannon Bldg., #124
Washington, D.C. 20515

Ex-Sen. Howard Metzenbaum
4512 Foxhill Crescent NW
Washington, DC 20007

Kweisi Mfume
3000 Druid Park Drive
Baltimore, MD 21215

Ex-Rep. Bob Michael
1029 N. Glenwood Street
Peoria, IL 61606

Sen. Barbara Mikulski (MD)
Senate Hart Building #709
Washington, DC 20510

Rep. Patsy Mink (HI)
House Rayburn Bldg., #2135
Washington, D.C. 20515

Ex-Sen. George Mitchell
8280 Greensboro Drive
McLean, VA 22102

Ambassador Walter Mondale
2116 Irving Avenue So.
Minneapolis, MN 55405

Sen. Carol Moseley-Braum (IL)
Senate Hart Building #320
Washington, DC 20510

Sen. Daniel Moynihan (NY)
Senate Russell Building #464
Washington, DC 20510

President Hosni Mubarak
Royal Palace
Cairo, EGYPT

Sen. Frank Murkowowski (AK)
Senate Hart Building #706
Washington, DC 20510

Sen. Patty Murray (WA)
Senate Russell Building #111
Washington, DC 20510

N   N

Benjamin Netanyahu
38 Rehou King George
Tel Aviv 61231 ISRAEL

Sen. Don Nickles (OK)
Senate Hart Building #133
Washington, DC 20510

General Manuel A. Noriega
#38699-079
P.O. Box 979132
Miami, FL 33197

Sam Nunn
915 Main Street
Perry, GA 31060

O   O

Justice Sandra Day O'Connor
1 - 1st Street N.E.
Washington, DC 20543

Rep. David Obey (WI)
House Rayburn Building #2462
Washington, DC 20515

Pres. Adolf Ogi
Bundeshaus
300 Bern SWITZERLAND

P

Rep. Ron Packard (CA)
House Rayburn Building #2372
Washington, DC 20515

Princess Ashraf Pahlavi
12 Avenue Montaigne
75016, Paris, FRANCE

Reverend Ian Paisley
"The Parsonage"
17 Cyprus Avenue
Belfast BT5 5NT NORTHERN IRELAND

Rep Mike Papas (NJ)
House Cannon Bldg. #228
Washington, DC 20515

Gov. George Pataki (NY)
State Capital Bldg.
Albany, NY 12247

Gov. Paul E. Patton (KY)
State Capiton
Frankfort, KY 40601

Rep. Bill Paxon (NY)
House Rayburn Building #2436
Washington, DC 20515

Rep. Nancy Pelosi (CA)
House Rayburn Building #2457
Washington, DC 20515

Rep. Solomon P. Ortiz (TX)
Rayburn House Office Bldg. #2136
Washington, DC 20515

P

Sec. Federico Pena
3517 Sterling Avenue
Alexandria, VA 22304

Ex-Sen Charles Percy
1691-34th Street NW
Washington, DC 20007

Shimon Peres
10 Hayarkon Street, #3263
Tel-Aviv, 63571 ISRAEL

Mme. Isabel Peron
Moreto 3, Los Jeronimos
E-28014 Madrid, SPAIN

William Perry
8017 Rising Ridge Road
Bethesda, MD 20817

HRH Prince Philip
Buckingham Palace
London, ENGLAND

Donald Pickering
Back Court, Manor House
Eastleach, Glos. ENGLAND

Rep. Richard Pombo (LA)
Longworth House Office Bldg. #1519
Washington, DC 20515

Q
_____ Q

Ex-Vice Pres. Dan Quayle
6263 N. Scottsdale Road #292
Scottsdale, AZ 85250

Marilyn Tucker Quayle
6263 Scottsdale Road #292
Scottsdale, AZ 85250

R
_____ R

President Hashemi Rafsanjani
The Majlis
Tehran IRAN

President Fidel Ramos
Malacanang Palace
Manila, PHILIPPINES

Rep. Charles B. Rangel (NY)
House Rayburn Building #2354
Washington, DC 20515

Crown Prince Ranier II
Grimaldi Palace
Monte Carlo, MONACO

Nancy Reagan
668 St. Cloud Road
Los Angeles, CA 90077

Ex-Pres. Ronald Reagan
668 St. Cloud Road
Los Angeles, CA 90077

Chief Justice Wm. Rehnquist
111-2nd Street NE
Washington, DC 20002

Sec. Janet Reno
Department of Justice
Washington, DC 20530

Ex-Gov. Ann Richards
P.O. Box 684746
Austin, TX 78768

Bill Richardson
799 United Nation Plaza
New York, NY 10017

Sec. Richard W. Riley
Department of Education
Washington, DC 20202

Mayor Richard Riordan
200 North Spring Street
Los Angeles, CA 90012

Sen. Charles Robb (VA)
Senate Russell Building #154
Washington, DC 20510

Sen. John Rockefeller (WV)
Senate Hart Building #109
Washington, DC 20510

Ex-Rep. Dan Rostenkowski
1372 West Evergreen Avenue
Chicago, IL 60622

Sec. Robert Rubin
Department of Treasury
Washington, DC 20220

S   S

Mme. Jehan El-Sadat
2310 Decatur Place N.W.
Washington, DC 20008

Saltan Hassanal Bokiah
Hassanal Bolkiah Nuda
Bandar Seri Begawan, BRUNEI

HRH Sarah, Dutchess Of York
Sunninghill Park
Windsor, Berks. ENGLAND

Justice Antonin Scalia
6713 Wemberly Way
McLean, VA 22101

Phyllis Schlafly
68 Fairmont
Alton, IL 62002

Mayor Kurt Schmoke
City Hall, 100 Holliday Street
Baltimore, MD 21201

Patricia Schroeder
c/o Assoc. of Amer. Publishers
71 - 5th Avenue
New York, NY 10003

Rep. Charles Schumer (NY)
House Rayburn Building #2211
Washington, DC 20515

Gen. Brent Scowcroft
6114 Wynnwood Road
Bethesda, MD 20816

Sec. Donna Shalala
Health and Human Services
200 Independence Avenue SW
Washington, DC 20201

Gen. John Shalikashvili
The Pentagon, Room 2E872
Washington, DC 20301

Sen. Richard Shelby (AL)
Senate Hart Building #110
Washington, DC 20510

Eduard Shevardnadze
State Council
Tbilisi GEORGIA

R. Sargent Shriver
1325 "G" Street, NW
Washington, DC 20005

Ex-Sen. Paul Simon
Southern Illinois University
Carbondale, IL 62901

Sec. Rodney Slater
Department of Transportation
Washington, DC 20590

Star Guide 1999-2000 Politics

Sen. Olympia Snowe (ME)
Senate Russell Building #495
Washington, DC 20510

Ted Sorenson
1285 Avenue of the Americas
New York, NY 10019

Justice David Souter
1 - 1st Street N.E.
Washington, DC 20543

Sen. Arlen Specter (PA)
Senate Hart Building #530
Washington, DC 20510

Princess Stephanie
Maison Clos St. Martin
F-St. Remy de Provence FRANCE

George Stephanopoulos
1717 De Sales Street NW
Washington, DC 20036

Sen. Ted Stevens (AK)
Senate Hart Building #522
Washington, DC 20510

Ex-Sen Adlai Stevenson III
10 South LaSalle Street, #3610
Chicago, IL 60604

Vice Adm. James Stockdale
Hoover Institute
Stanford, CA 94305

Rep. Louis Stokes (OH)
Rayburn, Hse. Office Bldg. #2365
Washington, DC 20515

Robert Strauss
1333 New Hampshire Ave. NW #400
Washington, DC 20036

John Sununu
24 Samoset Drive
Salem, NH 03079

T   T

Amb. Shirley Temple (Black)
115 Lakeview Drive
Woodside, CA 94062

Baroness Margaret Thatcher
Chester Square, Belgravia
London, ENGLAND

Justice Clarence Thomas
1 - 1st Street N.E.
Washington, DC 20543

Sen. Fred Thompson (IL)
701 Pennsylvania Avenue NW
Washington, DC 20004

Gov. Tommy Thompson
P.O. Box 7863
Madison, WI 53707

Sen. Strom Thurmond (SC)
Senate Russell Building #217
Washington, DC 20510

Kathleen Kennedy Townsend
100 State Circle
Annapolis, MD 21401

Archbishop Desmond Tutu
7981 Orlando West
Box 1131
Johannesburg, SOUTH AFRICA

U   U

Ex-Rep. Morris K. Udall
142 Calle Chaparita
Tucson, AZ 85716

Rep. Fred Upton (MI)
House Rayburn Building #2333
Washington, DC 20515

V   V

Cyrus Vance
425 Lexington Avenue
New York, NY 10017

Rep. Bruce Vento
Rayburn House Office Bldg. #2304
Washington, DC 20515

Rep. Nydia Velazquez (NY)
Cannon House Office Bldg. #132
Washington, DC 20515

Gov. George Voinovich (OH)
Office of the Governor
Columbus, OH 43266

W   W

Kurt Waldheim
1 Lobkowitz Platz
1010 Vienna, AUSTRIA

John Walsh
5151 Wisconsin Avenue, NW
Washington, DC 20016

Lech Walesa
Polskistr 53
Gdansk, POLAND

Sen. John Warner (VA)
Senate Russell Building #225
Washington, DC 20510

Ex-Gov. George Wallace
P.O. Box 667
Montgomery, AL 36101

Rep. Maxine Waters (CA)
Rayburn House Office Bldg. #2344
Washington, DC 20515

James G. Watt
P.O. Box 3705
Jackson Hole, WY 83001

Rep. J.C. Watts, Jr. (OK)
House Longworth Building #1713
Washington, DC 20515

Rep. Henry Waxman (CA)
House Rayburn Building #2204
Washington, DC 20515

Gov. William Weld (MA)
State Capitol, Room #373
Boston, MA 02135

Sen. Paul Wellstone (MN)
Senate Hart Building #717
Washington, DC 20510

Gen. William Westmoreland
107 1/2 Tradd St.
Box 1059
Charleston, SC 29401

Ex-Justice Byron White
6801 Hampshire Road
McLean, VA 22101

Prince William
Highgrove House
Gloucestershire ENGLAND

Gov. Pete Wilson (CA)
Office of the Governor, State Captol
Sacramento, CA 95814

Ex-Rep. James Wright, Jr.
Lanham Federal Building
819 Taylor Street, #9A10
Ft. Worth, TX 76102

Y-Z   Y-Z

Boris Yeltsin
Uliza Twerskaya
Jamskaya 2 Moscow RUSSIA

Ex-Mayor Sam Yorty
12797 Blairwood Drive
Studio City, CA 91604

Ex-Mayor Andrew Young
1088 Veltrie Circle S.W.
Atlanta, GA 30311

President Ernesto Zedillo
Presidencia Palacio Nacional
Mexico City DF 06220 MEXICO

Others

They're Not A Star Until
They're A Star In Star Guide™

A _____ A

Leslie Abramson
4929 Wilshire Blvd.
Los Angeles, CA 90010

Red Adair
P.O. Box 747
Bellville, TX 77418

Richard Adams
26 Church Street
Whitechurch, Hants., ENGLAND

Louis Adler
3969 Villa Costera
Malibu, CA 90265

Roger Ailes
440 Park Avenue South
New York, NY 10016

Edward Albee
P.O. Box 697
Montauk, NY 11954

Ginger Alden
6554 Whitetail Lane
Memphis, TN 38115

Dr. Edwin "Buzz" Aldrin
838 N. Doheny Drive #1407
West Hollywood, CA 90069

Kim Alexis
345 North Maple Drive #185
Beverly Hills, CA 90210

Mehmet Ali Agca
Rebibbia Prison
Rome ITALY

Gloria Allred
6300 Wilshire Blvd. #1500
Los Angeles, CA 90048

Hollis Alpert
P.O. Box 142
Shelter Island, NY 11964

Robert Altman
502 Park Avenue #15G
New York, NY 10022

Christiane Amanpour
25 rue de Ponthieu
75008 Paris FRANCE

Rodney Amateau
133 1/2 S. Linden Drive
Beverly Hills, CA 90212

Aldrich Ames
P.O. Box 3000
White Deer, PA 17887

Rachel Ames
303 S. Crescent Heights Blvd.
Los Angeles, CA 90048

Cleveland Amory
200 W. 57th Street
New York, NY 10019

Brad Anderson
13022 Wood Harbour Drive
Montgomery, TX 77356

Jack Anderson
7810 Kachina Lane
Potomac, MD 20854

Terry Anderson
50 Rockefeller Plaza
New York, NY 10020

Maya Angelou
3240 Valley Road
Winston-Salem, NC 28106

Wallis Annenberg
10273 Century Woods Place
Los Angeles, CA 90067

Army Archerd
442 Hilgard Avenue
Los Angeles, CA 90024

Ted Arison
3915 Biscayne Blvd.
Miami, FL 33137

Samuel Z. Arkoff
3205 Oakdell Lane
Studio City, CA 91604

Roone Arledge
1330 Avenue of the Americas
New York, NY 10019

Giorgio Armani
Palazzo Durini 24
I-20122 Milan ITALY

Garner Ted Armstrong
P.O. Box 2525
Tyler, TX 75710

Neil Armstrong
777 Columbus Avenue
Lebanon, OH 45036

Mary Kay Ash
16251 Dallas Parkway
Dallas, TX 75248

Richard Avedon
407 East 75th Street
New York, NY 10021

B   B

Don Bachardy
145 Adelaide Drive
Santa Monica, CA 90402

Max Baer, Jr.
3455 Eastern Avenue
Las Vegas, NV 89109

F. Lee Bailey
1400 Centre Park Blvd. #909
West Palm Beach, FL 33401

Beryl Bainbridge
42 Albert Street
London NW1 7NU ENGLAND

Jim Bakker
P.O. Box 1007
Hendersonville, NC 28793

Tammy Faye Bakker
72727 Country Club Drive
Rancho Mirage, CA 92270

Tyra Banks
9800 South 2nd Avenue
Inglewood, CA 90305

Joseph Barbera
12003 Briarvale Lane
Studio City, CA 91604

Dr. Christian Barnard
Box 6143, Weigmoed
Capetown 7583 SOUTH AFRICA

Barney
P.O. Box 8000
Allen, TX 75002

Mikhail Baryshnikov
157 West 57th Street #502
New York, NY 10019

Alan Bean
9173 Briar Forest Drive
Houston, TX 77024

Marilyn Beck
P.O. Box 11079
Beverly Hills, CA 90213

Saul Bellow
1126 East 59th Street
Chicago, IL 60637

Peter Bencheley
35 Boudinot Street
Princeton, NJ 08540

William Bennett
20 West Lenox Street
Chevy Chase, MD 20815

Ingmar Bergman
P.O. Box 27127
S-10252 Stockholm, SWEDEN

David Berkowitz #78A1976
Sullivan Correctional Facility
Box AG
Fallsburg, NY 12733

Jay Bernstein
9360 Beverly Crest Drive
Beverly Hills, CA 90210

Mr. Blackwell
531 South Windsor Blvd.
Los Angeles, CA 90005

Nina Blanchard
3610 Wrightwood Drive
Studio City, CA 91604

Bill Blass
550 - 7th Avenue
New York, NY 10019

Linda Bloodworth-Thompson
4000 Warner Blvd. Bldg. #147
Burbank, CA 91505

Betsy Bloomingdale
131 Delfern Drive
Los Angeles, CA 90077

Judy Blume
40 E. 48th Street #1001
New York, NY 10017

John Wayne Bobbitt
7226 Westpark Avenue
Las Vegas, NV 89117

Lorena Bobbitt
709 Gray Avenue
Durham, NC 27701

Charley Boorman
Glebe, Annanoe County
Wicklow, IRELAND

Robert Bork
5171 Palisade Lane
Washington, DC 20016

Barbara Taylor Bradford
425 East 58th Street
New York, NY 10022

Benjamin Bradlee
3014 "N" Street NW
Washington, DC 20007

Christie Brinkley
344 East 59th Street
New York, NY 10022

David Brinkley
111 East Melrose Street
Chevy Chase, MD 20815

Edgar Bronfman
375 Park Avenue
New York, NY 10152

Dr. Joyce Brothers
235 East 45th Street
New York, NY 10017

Helen Gurley Brown
One West 81st Street #220
New York, NY 10024

Anita Bryant
P.O. Box 7300
Branson, MO 65615

Art Buchwald
4327 Hawthorne Street NW
Washington, DC 20016

William F. Buckley, Jr.
150 E. 35th Street
New York, NY 10016

Warren Buffett
3555 Farnam Street
Omaha, NE 68131

Vincent T. Bugliosi
1926 W. Mountain Street
Glendale, CA 91201

Ken Burns
Maple Grove Road
Walpole, NH 03608

Joey Buttafuoco
P.O. Box 335
Agoura Hills, CA 91376

Dick Button
250 W. 57th Street #1818
New York, NY 10107

C _____ C

Lt. William Calley
c/o V.V. Vicks Jewelry
Cross Country Plaza
Columbus, GA 31903

James Cameron
919 Santa Monica Blvd.
Santa Monica, CA 90401

Naomi Campbell
107 Greene Street
New York, NY 10012

Stephen Cannell
1220 Hillcrest
Pasadena, CA 91106

Pierre Cardin
59 Rue du Faubourg
St. Honore
F-75008 Paris, FRANCE

A.J. Carothers
2110 The Terrace
Los Angeles, CA 90049

Scott Carpenter
P.O. Box 3161
Vail, CO 81658

Allan Carr
1203 N. Sweezer #101
West Hollywood, CA 90069

Hodding Carter III
211 South St. Asaph
Alexandria, VA 22314

Barbara Cartland
Camfield Place Hatfield
Hertfordshire AL9 6JE, ENGLAND

Oleg Cassini
3 West 57th Street
New York, NY 10019

Engene Cernan
7 Windemere
Houston, TX 77063

Charles Champlin
2169 Linda Flora Drive
Los Angeles, CA 90024

Mark David Chapman
#81 A 3860, Box 149
Attica Correctional Facility
Attica, NY 14011

Suzette Charles
3680 Madrid Street
Las Vegas, NV 89121

Benjamin Chavis
P.O. Box 1661
Ellicott City, MD 21041

Julia Child
103 Irving Street
Cambridge, MA 02138

Deepak Chopra
948 Granvis Altamira
Palos Verdes, CA 90274

Michael Cimino
9015 Alto Cedro
Beverly Hills, CA 90210

Liz Claiborne
650 Fifth Avenue
New York, NY 10019

Mary Higgins Clark
210 Central Park South
New York, NY 10019

Arthur C. Clarke
4715 Gregory's Road
Colombo SRI LANKA

Johnnie Cochran, Jr.
2373 Hobart Blvd.
Los Angeles, CA 90027

Jackie Collins
616 N. Beverly Drive
Beverly Hills, CA 90210

Marva Collins
4146 West Chicago Avenue
Chicago, IL 60651

Charles (Chuck) Colson
P.O. Box 97103
Washington, DC 20090

Charles T. Conrad, Jr.
6301 Princeville Circle
Huntington Beach, CA 92648

Christian Conrad
21006 Dumetz Road
West Hills, CA 91364

Kimbery Conrad
10236 Charing Cross Road
Los Angeles, CA 90077

Paul Conrad
28649 Crestridge Road
Palos Verdes, CA 90274

Dr. Denton Cooley
3014 Del Monte Drive
Houston, TX 77019

Lt. Col. L. Gordon Cooper
5011 Woodley Avenue
Encino, CA 91436

David Copperfield
515 Post Oak Blvd. #300
Houston, TX 77027

Francis Coppola
916 Kearny Street
San Francisco, CA 91433

Roger Corman
2501 La Mesa Drive
Santa Monica, CA 90402

Norman Corwin
1840 Fairburn Avenue #302
Los Angeles, CA 90025

Jenny Craig
P.O. Box 387190
La Jolla, CA 92038

Cindy Crawford
132 S. Rodeo Drive, #300
Beverly Hills, CA 90212

Michael Crichton
433 N. Camden Drive #500
Beverly Hills, CA 90210

Judith Crist
180 Riverside Drive
New York, NY 10024

Walter Cronkite
870 United Nations Plaza #25A
New York, NY 10017

Norm Crosby
1400 Londonderry Place
Los Angeles, CA 90069

D   D

The Dalai Lama
Thekchen Choling
McLeod Gundi, Kangra
Himachal Pradesh, INDIA

Abby Dalton
P.O. Box 100
Mammoth Lakes, CA 93546

Joe Dante
3176 Lindo Street
Los Angeles, CA 90068

Christopher Darden
675 So. Westmoreland Avenue
Los Angeles, CA 90005

Prof. Angela Davis
4400 Keller Avenue #260-174
Oakland, CA 94506

Gen. Benjamin O. Davis
1001 Wilson Blvd. #906
Arlington, VA 22209

Jim Davis
450 Country Road
New Albany, IN 47320

John Dean
9496 Rembert Lane
Beverly Hills, CA 90210

Hubert De Givenchy
3 Avenue George V
75008, Paris, FRANCE

Oscar De La Renta
Brook Hill Farm
Skiff Mountain Road
Kent, CT 06757

Dino De Laurentiis
Via Poutina Ku 23270
Rome, ITALY

John Z. DeLorean
567 Lamington Road
Bedminster, NJ 07921

Reginald Denny
844 North Vernon Avenue
Azusa, CA 91702

Brian De Palma
5555 Melrose Avenue
Ernst Lubitch Annex, #119
Los Angeles, CA 90038

Alan Dershowitz
1563 Massachusetts Avenue
Cambridge, MA 02138

Barry Diller
1365 Enterprise Drive
West Chester, PA 19280

Christian Dior
St.Anna Platz 2
80538 Munich GERMANY

Roy Disney
500 S. Buena Vista
Burbank, CA 91521

Alan Drury
P.O. Box 647
Tiburon, CA 94920

Dominick Dunne
155 East 49th Street
New York, NY 10017

E   E

Roger Ebert
P.O. Box 146366
Chicago, IL 60614

Michael Eisner
500 S. Buena Vista
Burbank, CA 91521

Linda Ellerbee
96 Morton Street
New York, NY 10014

Linda Evangelista
2640 Carmen Crest Drive
Los Angeles, CA 90068

F   F

Fabio
P.O. Box 4
Inwood, NY 11696

Rev. Jerry Falwell
P.O. Box 6004
Forest, VA 24551

Min. Louis Farrakhan
4855 South Woodlawn Avenue
Chicago, IL 60615

Jules Feiffer
RR #1, Box 440
Vineyard Haven, MA 02568

Cristina Ferrare
1280 Stone Canyon Road
Los Angeles, CA 90077

Bobby Fischer
186 Rt. 9-W
New Windsor, NY 12250

Amy Fisher
3595 State School Road
Albion, NY 14411

Mary Fisher
3075 Hampton Place
Boco Raton, FL 33434

Larry Flynt
9211 Robin Drive
Los Angeles, CA 90069

Ken Follett
P.O. Box 708
London SW10 0DH ENGLAND

Steve Forbes
60 Fifth Avenue
New York, NY 10011

Eileen Otte Ford
344 E. 59th Street
New York, NY 10022

Milos Forman
The Hampshire House
150 Central Park Square
New York, NY 10019

John Fowles
52 Floral Street
London, WC2, ENGLAND

Milton Friedman
Quadrangle Office
Hoover Institute
Stanford University
Palo Alto, CA 94305

Lynette "Squeaky" Fromme
#00060750-180, FCI,
Shawnee Unit, Box 7006
Marianna, FL 32447

Daisy Fuentes
2200 Fletcher Avenue
Ft. Lee, NJ 07024

Mark Fuhrman
P.O. Box 141
Sandpoint, ID 83864

G   G

John Kenneth Galbraith
30 Francis Avenue
Cambridge, MA 02138

Dr. George Gallup II
The Great Road
Princeton, NJ 08540

Daryl Gates
756 Portola Terrace
Los Angeles, CA 90042

William "Bill" Gates
1 Microsoft Way
Redmond, WA 98052

Uri Geller
Sonning-on-Thames
Berkshire ENGLAND

Phyllis George
Cave Hill - Box 4308
Lexington, KY 40503

Mrs. J. Paul Getty
1535 N. Beverly Drive
Beverly Hills, CA 90210

Hubert Givency
3 Avenue George V
75008 Paris FRANCE

Bernhard Goetz
55 W. 14th Street
New York, NY 10011

Fred Goldman
P.O. Box 6016
Agoura Hills, CA 91376

William Goldman
50 E. 77th Street #30
New York, NY 10021

Samuel Goldwyn, Jr.
10203 Santa Monica Blvd. #500
Los Angeles, CA 90067

Jane Goodall
P.O. Box 41720
Tucson, AZ 85717

John Gotti #18261-053
Rt. 5, Box 2000
Marion, IL 629590

Lord Lew Grade
8 Queen Street
London, W1X 7PH, ENGLAND

Rev. Billy Graham
P.O. Box 779
Minneapolis, MN 55440

Katherine Graham
2920 "R" Street N.W.
Washington, DC 20007

Earl G. Graves
130 Fifth Avenue
New York, NY 10011

Ex-Rep. William Gray III
500 East 62nd Street
New York, NY 10021

Graham Greene
121 North San Vicente Blvd.
Beverly Hills, CA 90211

Dick Gregory
P.O. Box 3270
Plymouth, MA 02361

Merv Griffin
9876 Wilshire Blvd.
Beverly Hills, CA 90210

John Grisham
P.O. Box 1156
Oxford, MS 38655

George Grizzard
400 East 54th Street
New York, NY 10022

Bob Guccione
277 Park Avenue
New York, NY 10017

Cathy Guisewite
4900 Main Street
Kansas City, MO 64112

H   H

Jessica Hahn
6345 Balboa Blvd., #375
Encino, CA 91316

Arthur Hailey
Box N7776, Lyford Cay
Nassau, BAHAMAS

Jack Haley, Jr.
1443 Devlin Drive
Los Angeles, CA 90069

Fawn Hall
1568 Viewsite Drive
Los Angeles, CA 90069

Jerry Hall
304 West 81st Street
New York, NY 10024

Holly Hallstrom
5750 Wilshire Blvd. #475W
Los Angeles, CA 90036

Billy James Hargis
Rose of Sharon Farm
Neosho, MO 64840

Mrs. Jean Harris
c/o General Delivery
Monroe, NH 03771

Paul Harvey
1035 Park Avenue
River Forest, IL 60305

Patricia Hearst
110 - 5th Street
San Francisco, CA 94103

Mrs. Wm. Randolph Hearst
875 Comstock Avenue #16B
Los Angeles, CA 90024

Christie Hefner
680 N. Lake Avenue
Chicago, IL 60611

Hugh Hefner
10236 Charing Cross Road
Los Angeles, CA 90024

Leona Helmsley
36 Central Park South
New York, NY 10019

Heloise
P.O. Box 795000
San Antonio, TX 78279

Don Hewitt
555 W. 57th Street
New York, NY 10019

Thor Heyerdahl
E-38500 Guimar
(Tenerife) SPAIN

Jack Higgins
Septembertide
Mont DeLa Rocque
Jersey, Channel Islands (U.K.)

Tommy Hilfiger
25 West 39th Street #1300
New York, NY 10018

Anita Hill
300 Timberdell Road
Norman, OK 73019

Sir Edmund Hillary
278A Remuera Road
Auckland, SE2, NEW ZEALAND

Baron Hilton
28775 Sea Ranch Way
Malibu, CA 90265

John Hinckley, Jr.
St. Elizabeth's Hospital
2700 Martin L. King Avenue
Washington, DC 20005

James Hoffa, Jr.
2593 Hounds Chase Drive
Troy, MI 48096

Syd Hoffs
P.O. Box 2463
Miami Beach, FL 33140

Benjamin Hooks
260 Fifth Avenue
New York, NY 10001

Mrs. Dolores Hope
10346 Moorpark North
North Hollywood, CA 91602

Arianna Huffington
3005-45th Street NW
Washington, DC 20016

Lamar Hunt
1601 Elm Street #2800
Dallas, TX 75021

Rachel Hunter
23 Beverly Park
Beverly Hills, CA 90210

Elizabeth Hurley
3 Cromwell Place
London SW 2JE ENGLAND

Joe Hyams
10375 Wilshire Blvd. #4D
Los Angeles, CA 90024

I _____ I

Lee Iacocca
30 Scenic Oaks
Bloomfield Hills, MI 48013

Iman
111 East 22nd Street #200
New York, NY 10010

Kathy Ireland
P.O. Box 5353
Santa Barbara, CA 93130

Judge Lance Ito
825 So. Madison Avenue
Pasadena, CA 91106

J   J

LaToya Jackson
14126 Rosecrans Avenue
Santa Fe Springs, CA 90670

Bianca Jagger
530 Park Avenue #18D
New York, NY 10021

Norman Jewison
3000 W. Olympic Blvd. #1314
Santa Monica, CA 90404

Joyce Jillson
64 E. Concord Street
Orlando, FL 32801

Steve Jobs
900 Chesapeake Drive
Redwood City, CA 94063

Paula Jones
1 Third Place
Long Beach, CA 90802

K   K

Brian "Kato" Kaelin
8383 Wilshire Blvd. #954
Beverly Hills, CA 90211

Donna Karan
550-7th Avenue #1500
New York, NY 10018

Yousuf Karsh
1 Rideau Street
Ottawa Ontario
K1N 9S7 CANADA

Lawrence Kasdan
10345 W. Olympic Blvd.
Los Angeles, CA 90064

Kitty Kelly
3037 Dunbarton Avenue N.W,
Washington, DC 20007

Caroline Kennedy-Schlossberg
641 - 6th Avenue
New York, NY 10011

John Kennedy, Jr.
20 N. Moore Street
New York, NY 10013

Leon Isaac Kennedy
9427 Via Monique
Burbank, CA 91504

Kirk Kerkorian
4835 Koval Lane
Las Vegas, NV 89109

Dr. Jack Kevorkian
4870 Lockhart Street
West Bloomfield, MI 48323

Ted Key
1694 Glenhardie Road
Wayne, PA 19087

Victor K. Kiam II
60 Main Street
Bridgeport, CT 06602

Rodney King
9100 Wilshire Blvd. #250-W
Beverly Hills, CA 90212

Stephen King
47 West Broadway
Bangor, ME 04401

Gelsey Kirkland
191 Silver Moss Drive
Vero Beach, FL 32963

Calvin Klein
205 W. 39th Street
New York, NY 10018

Dean R. Koontz
P.O. Box 9529
Newport Beach, CA 92658

Dr. C. Everett Koop
5924 Maplewood Park Place
Bethesda, MD 20814

Stanley Kramer
2530 Shira Drive
Valley Village, CA 91607

Kreskin
P.O. Box 1383
West Caldwell, NJ 07006

William Kristol
6625 Jill Court
McLean, VA 22101

Mrs. Joan Kroc
8939 Villa La Jolla Drive
La Jolla, CA 92037

L   L

Alan Ladd, Jr.
312 North Faring Road
Los Angeles, CA 90077

Dr. Arthur Laffer
5375 Executive Square #330
La Jolla, CA 92037

Melvin Laird
1730 Rhode Island Avenue NW
Washington, DC 20036

Sir Freddie Laker
138 Cheapside
London EC2V 6BL ENGLAND

Ann Landers
435 N. Michigan Avenue
Chicago, IL 60611

John Landis
9402 Beverly Crest Drive
Beverly Hills, CA 90210

Sherry Lansing
10451 Bellagio Road
Los Angeles, CA 90077

Ring Lardner, Jr.
55 Central Park West
New York, NY 10023

Gary Larson
4900 Main Street #900
Kansas City, MO 62114

Fred Lasswell
1111 N. Westshore Blvd. #604
Tampa, FL 33607

Estee Lauder
767 Fifth Avenue
New York, NY 10153

Ralph Lauren
1107 - 5th Avenue
New York, NY 10128

Arthur Laurents
P.O. Box 582
Quoque, NY 11959

Norman Lear
1999 Avenue of the Stars, #500
Los Angeles, CA 90067

John Le Carre
9 Gainsborough Gardens
London NW3 1BJ ENGLAND

Spike Lee
40 Acres & A Mule Film Works
124 De Kalb Avenue #2
Brooklyn, NY 11217

Elmore Leonard
2192 Yarmouth Road
Bloomfield Village, MI 48301

Ira Levin
425 Madison Avenue
New York, NY 10017

Monica Lewinsky
C/O Marcia Lewis
700 New Hampshire Avenue, NW.
Washington, DCC 20037

Shari Lewis
603 N. Alta Drive
Beverly Hills, CA 90210

G. Gordon Liddy
9112 Riverside Drive
Ft. Washington, MD 20744

Rush Limbaugh
366 Madison Avenue #700
New York, NY 10177

Ann Morrow Lindbergh
P.O. Box 157
Peacham, VT 05682

Jack R. Lousma
2722 Roseland Street
Ann Arbor, MI 48103

James A. Lovell
5725 E. River Road
Chicago, IL 60611

George Lucas
P.O. Box 2459
San Rafael, CA 94912

Robert Ludlum
P.O. Box 235
Bedford Hills, NY 10507

Sidney Lumet
1 West 81st Street
New York, NY 10024

M   M

Elle MacPherson
414 East 52nd Street PH B
New York, NY 10022

Garry Marshall
10459 Sarah Street
Toluca Lake, CA 91602

Norman Mailer
142 Columbia Heights
Brooklyn, NY 11201

Mary Matalin
P.O. Box 18686
Washington, DC 20036

John Malone
4643 South Ulster
Denver, CO 80237

Septuplets McCaughey
615 North First
Carlisle, IA 50047

Leonard Maltin
10424 Whipple Street
Touca Lake, CA 91602

Sarah McClendon
3133 Connecticut Avenue NW #215
Washington, DC 20008

David Mamet
P.O. Box 381589
Cambridge, MA 02238

Julie McCullough
8033 Sunset Blvd. #353
Los Angeles, CA 90046

William Manchester
Westleyan Station
P.O. Box 329
Middleton, CT 06457

James McDivitt
9146 Cherry Avenue
Rapid City, MI 49676

Rod McKuen
1155 Angelo Drive
Beverly Hills, CA 90210

Charles Manson #B33920
Pelican Bay State Prison
5905 Lake Earl Drive
Crescent City, CA 95531

Susan Carpenter McMillan
1744 Oak Lane
San Marino, CA 91108

Forrest Mars
6885 Elm Street
McLean, VA 22101

Terrence McNally
218 W. 10th Street
New York, NY 10014

Robert McNamara
2412 Tracy Place NW
Washington, DC 20008

Timothy McVeigh, #12076-064
9595 W. Quincy Avenue
Littleton, CO 80123

Edwin Meese III
1075 Springhill Road
McLean, VA 22102

Eric Menendez #1878449
CSP-Sac., Box 290066
Represa, CA 95671

Lyle Menendez #1887106
California Correctional Institute
CCI-Box 1031
Tehachapi, CA 93581

Russ Meyer
3121 Arrowhead Drive
Los Angeles, CA 90068

Lorne Michaels
88 Central Park West
New York, NY 10023

Michael Milken
4543 Tara Drive
Encino, CA 91436

Arthur Miller
RR 1, Box 320 - Tophet Road
Roxbury, CT 06783

Marvin Mitchelson
2500 Apollo Drive
Los Angeles, CA 90046

Thomas L. Monaghan
3001 Earhart
Ann Arbor, MI 48106

Rev. Sun Myung Moon
4 W. 43rd Street
New York, NY 10010

Dick Morris
20 Beeholm Road
West Redding, CT 06896

Toni Morrison
185 Nassau Street
Princeton, NJ 08544

Mother Delores (Debra Hart)
Regina Laudis Convent
Bethlehem, CT 06751

Stewart Mott
515 Madison Avenue
New York, NY 10022

The Muppets
P.O. Box 20726
New York, NY 10023

Rupert Murdoch
1211 - 6th Avenue
New York, NY 10036

Dee Dee Myers
30 Rockefeller Plaza
New York, NY 10112

N   N

Ralph Nader
1600-20th Street NW
Washington, DC 20009

Hal Needham
2220 Avenue of the Stars #302
Los Angeles, CA 90067

LeRoy Neiman
One W. 67th Street
New York, NY 10023

Samuel I. Newhouse, Jr.
950 Fingerboard Road
Staten Island, NY 10305

Lynn Nofziger
2000 Pennsylvania Ave. NW #365
Washington, DC 20037

Dr. Thomas Noguchi
1110 Avoca Avenue
Pasadena, CA 91105

Oliver North
P.O. Box 9771
McLean, VA 22102

Robert Novak
1750 Pennsylvania Ave. NW #1312
Washington, DC 20006

O   O

Patrick Oliphant
4900 Main Street, 9th Floor
Kansas City, MO 64112

Sydner Omarr
201 Ocean Avenue #1706B
Santa Monica, CA 90402

Athina Onassis
88 Avenue Foch
75016 Paris, FRANCE

Marcel Ophuls
10 rue Ernst-Deloison
92200 Neuilly FRANCE

Yuri Orlov
Cornell University
Newman Laboratory
Ithaca, NY 14853

Nagisa Osima
4-11-5 Kugenuma-Matsugaoka
Fujisawa-Shi 251 JAPAN

Michael Ovitz
9465 Wilshire Blvd., #750
Beverly Hills, CA 90212

Frank Oz
P.O. Box 20750
New York, NY 10023

P   P

Camilla Parker-Bowles
Ray Mill House, Reybridege. nr.
Chippenham, Wiltshire ENGLAND

Rosa Parks
9336 Wildemere Street
Detroit, MI 48206

I.M. Pei
600 Madison Avenue
New York, NY 10022

H. Ross Perot
1700 Lakeside Square
Dallas, TX 75251

Roman Polanski
43 Avenue Montaigne
75008, Paris, FRANCE

Sidney Pollack
13525 Lucca Drive
Pacific Palisades, CA 90272

Pope John Paul II
Palazzo Apostolico Vaticano
Vatican City, ITALY

Paula Poundstone
1223 Broadway #162
Santa Monica, CA 90404

Gen. Colin L. Powell
909 N. Washington Street #767
Alexandria, VA 22314

Lisa-Marie Presley
1167 Summit Drive
Beverly Hills, CA 90210

Wolfgang Puck
805 N. Sierra Drive
Beverly Hills, CA 90210

Mario Puzo
866 Manor Lane
Bay Shore, NY 11706

R   R

Mrs. Lea Rabin
Rehov Abba Hillel 14, 15th Floor
Ramat-Gun ISRAEL

Ralph Read
P.O. Box 1990
Chesapeake, VA 23327

Sumner Redstone
200 Elm Street
Dedham, MA 02026

Rex Reed
1 W. 72nd Street #86
New York, NY 10023

Faye Resnick
301 North Canon Drive #203
Beverly Hills, CA 90210

Matty Rich
9560 Wilshire Blvd. #500
Beverly Hills, CA 90212

Dr. Sally Ride
9500 Gillman Drive
MS 0221
La Jolla, CA 92093

Cokie Roberts
5315 Bradley Blvd.
Bethesda, MD 20814

Oral Roberts
7777 Lewis Street
Tulsa, OK 74130

Pat Robertson
Christian Broadcasting
1000 Centerville Turnpike
Virgina Beach, VA 23463

Randall Robinson
1744 "R" Street, NW
Washington, DC 20009

Chris Rock
527 North Azusa Avenue #231
Covina, CA 91722

David Rockefeller, Jr.
30 Rockefeller Plaza #506
New York, NY 10112

Mrs. Nelson Rockefeller
812 Fifth Avenue
New York, NY 10021

Ed Rollins
510 King Street, #302
Alexandria, VA 22314

Carl T. Rowan
3116 Fessenden Street VW
Washington, DC 20008

Salman Rushdie
c/o Gillon Aitken
29 Fernshaw Road
London SW10 OTG ENGLAND

Mark Russell
3201 - 33rd Plaza, NW
Washington, DC 20008

S   S

J.D. Salinger
R.R. #3, Box 176
Cornish Flat, NH 03746

Pierre Salinger
3114 "O" Street NW
Washington, DC 20007

Vincent Sardi, Jr.
234 W. 44th Street
New York, NY 10036

Vidal Sassoon
1163 Calle Vista
Beverly Hills, CA 90210

Francesco Scavullo
216 E. 63rd Street
New York, NY 10021

Claudia Schiffer
5 Union Square #500
New York, NY 10003

Walter M. Schirra, Jr.
16834 Via de Santa Fe
Rancho Santa Fe, CA 92067

Arthur Schlesinger, Jr.
33 W. 42nd Street
New York, NY 10036

Dr. Laura Schlessinger
610 South Ardmore Avenue
Los Angeles, CA 90005

Daniel Schorr
3113 Woodley Road
Washington, DC 20008

Gen. Norman Schwarzkopf
400 North Ashley Drive #3050
Tampa, FL 33609

Martin Scorsese
445 Park Avenue #700
New York, NY 10022

Bobby Seale
302 West Chelton Avenue
Philadelphia, PA 19144

Erich Segal
53 the Pryors
East Heath Road
London, NW3 1BP, ENGLAND

Stephanie Seymour
5415 Oberlin Drive
San Diego, CA 92121

Robert Shapiro
2590 Walingford Drive
Beverly Hills, CA 90210

Rev. Al Sharpton
1941 Madison Avenue #2
New York, NY 10035

Sidney Sheldon
10250 Sunset Blvd.
Los Angeles, CA 90077

Siegfried & Roy
1639 N. Valley Drive
Las Vegas, NV 89108

Fred Silverman
12400 Wilshire Blvd. #920
Los Angeles, CA 90025

Richard Simmons
P.O. Box 5403
Beverly Hills, CA 90209

Neil Simon
10745 Chalon Road
Los Angeles, CA 90077

John Singleton
P.O. Box 92547
Pasadena, CA 91107

Sirhan Sirhan
#B21014
Corcoran State Prison
P.O. Box 8800
Corcoran, CA 93212

Gene Siskel
1301 North Astor
Chicago, IL 60610

Eleanor Smeal
900 North Stafford Street #1217
Arlington, VA 22003

Yakov Smirnoff
1999 South Bundy Drive #200
Los Angeles, CA 90025

Liz Smith
160 E. 38th Street
New York, NY 10016

Susan Smith
#4901-1104-94
Women's Correctional Facility
4450 Broad River Road
Columbia, SC 29210

Lord Snowdon
22 Lauceston Place
London W1 ENGLAND

Alexander Solzhenitsyn
Plyushchikha Street
Moscow RUSSIA

Aaron Spelling
594 N. Mapleton Drive
Los Angeles, CA 90077

Gerry Spence
15 South Jackson
Jackson, WY 83001

Earl Charles Spencer
Althorpe House, Great Brington
Northamptonshire NN7 4HQ ENGLAND

Steven Spielberg
P.O. Box 8520
Universal City, CA 91608

Mickey Spillane
P.O. Box 265
Murrells Inlet, SC 29576

Kenneth Starr
333 Constitution Avenue, NW
Washington, DC 20001

Danielle Steel
P.O. Box 1637
Murray Hill Station
New York, NY 10156

Gloria Steinem
118 E. 73rd Street
New York, NY 10021

Howard Stern
40 West 57th Street #1400
New York, NY 10019

Martha Stewart
Lily Pond Lane
East Hampton, NY 11937

Oliver Stone
520 Broadway #600
Santa Monica, CA 90401

William Styron
12 Rucum Road
Roxbury, CT 06783

Jimmy Swaggert
8912 World Ministry Avenue
Baton Rouge, LA 70810

T   T

Gay Talese
154 E. Atlantic Blvd.
Ocean City, NJ 08226

Amy Tan
373 South Robertson Blvd.
Beverly Hills, CA 90211

Niki Taylor
8362 Pines Blvd., #334
Hollywood, FL 33024

Dr. Edward Teller
P.O. Box 808
Livermore, CA 94550

Studs Terkel
850 W. Castlewood
Chicago, IL 60640

Dave Thomas
4288 W. Dublin Granville Road
Dublin, OH 53017

Cheryl Tiegs
2 Greenwich Plaza #100
Greenwich, CT 06830

Robert Townsend
2934 1/2 N Beverly Glen Circle
Suite #407
Los Angeles, CA 90077

Linda Tripp
27285 Boyce Mill Road
Greensboro, MD 21639

Gary Trudeau
459 Columbus Avenue #113
New York, NY 10024

Donald Trump
721 Fifth Avenue
New York, NY 10022

Ivana Trump
500 Park Avenue #500
New York, NY 10022

Ted Turner
1050 Techwood Drive N.W.
Atlanta, GA 30318

Scott Turow
Sears Tower #8000
Chicago, IL 60606

U   U

John Updike
675 Hale Street
Beverly, MA 01915

Leon Uris
P.O. Box 1559
Aspen, CO 81611

V   V

Abigail Van Buren
P.O. Box 69440
Los Angeles, CA 90069

Bob Vila
10877 Wilshire Blvd. #900
Los Angeles, CA 90024

Mario Van Peebles
853 - 7th Avenue #3E
New York, NY 10019

Paul A. Volcker
Prof. International Economics
Princeton University
Princeton, NJ 08544

Gore Vidal
1201 Alta Loma Road
Los Angeles, CA 90069

Diane Von Furstenberg
389 West 12th Street
New York, NY 10014

Richard Viguerie
7777 Leesburg Pike
Falls Church, VA 22043

Kurt Vonnegut, Jr.
P.O. Box 27
Sagaponack, NY 11962

W   W

Alice Walker
327 - 25th Street #3
San Francisco, CA 94121

Andrew Lloyd Webber
Trump Tower
725 Fifth Avenue
New York, NY 10022

Mort Walker
61 Studio Court
Stamford, CT 06903

Casper W. Weinberger
700 New Hampshire Avenue NW
Washington, DC 20037

The Great Wallendas
138 Frog Hollow Road
Churchville, PA 18966

Dr. Ruth Westheimer
900 W. 190th Street
New York, NY 10040

John Waters
1018 North Charles Street
Baltimore, MD 21201

Heather Whitestone
P.O. Box 672801
Marietta, GA 30006

Elie Wiesel
745 Commonwealth Avenue
Boston, MA 02115

Simon Wiesenthal
Salvtorgasse 6
1010, Vienna, 1, AUSTRIA

George Will
9 Grafton Street
Chevy Chase, MD 20815

Kathleen Willey
2320 Castlebridge Road
Midlothian, VA 23113

Bruce Williams
P.O. Box 547
Elfers, FL 34680

Bob Woodward
2907 "Q" Street NW
Washington, DC 20007

Herman Wouk
303 Crestview
Palm Springs, CA 92264

Steve Wozniak
475 Alberto Way
Los Gatos, CA 95030

Y   Y

Mollie Yard
1000 - 16th Street N.W.
Washington, DC 20036

Gen. Charles E. Yeager
P.O. Box 128
Cedar Ridge, CA 95924

Z   Z

Richard Zanuck
202 N. Canon Drive
Beverly Hills, CA 90210

Franco Zefferelli
91 Regent Street
London W1R 7TB ENGLAND

Bob Zemeckis
1880 Century Park E., #900
Los Angeles, CA 90067

Ron Ziegler
2008 Fort Drive
Alexandria, VA 22307

Index

They're Not A Star Until
They're A Star In Star Guide™

MAKE CONTACT WITH THE STARS!

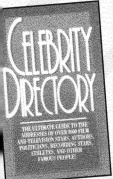

The **Celebrity Directory**™ **(9th Edition)** covers the entire spectrum of of celebrities. If a person is famous or worth locating, it's almost certain that their address can be found in the Celebrity Directory. ISBN 0-943213-31-2 **$39.95+$2.95 postage & handling.**

Use the **Celebrity Birthday Directory**™ **(4th Edition)** to find the birthdays of your favorite celebrities. Alphabetized for quick reference.
ISBN 0-943213-26-6
Only $10.95+$1.95 postage & handling

The **1999-2000 Star Guide**™ is the most reliable and up-to-date guide available for over 3200 addresses of major stars from every field.
ISBN 0-943213-30-4
Only $12.95+$1.95 postage & handling.

The **Celebrity Birthday Guide**™ **(4th Edition)** lists the birthdays of celebrities past and present. Thousands of entries by calendar date.
ISBN 0-943213-25-8
Only $10.95+$1.95 postage & handling.

Name_____

Address_____

City_____State_____Zip_____

____ Copies of **Celebrity Directory**™ @ $39.95 each + $2.95 P&H
____ Copies of **Celebrity Birthday Directory**™ @ $10.95 each + $1.95 P&H
____ Copies of **Star Guide**™ @ $12.95 each + $1.95 P&H
____ Copies of **Celebrity Birthday Guide**™ @ $10.95 each + $1.95 P&H
____ Copies of **The Marriage Book**™ @ $9.95 each + $1.95 P&H

Total Order $_____,_____

Star Guide-78¢
Celebrity Directory-$2.40
Celebrity Birthday Guide-66¢
Celebrity Birthday Directory-66¢

Total Postage & Handling $_____,_____

MI Residents add 6% Sales Tax * $_____,_____

Add $3.00 per item for 2nd DAY PRIORITY MAIL   Total Enclosed $_____,_____

The Marriage Book is a collection of words of wisdom every one should read before marrying.
ISBN 0-943213-26-6 LC#97-74584
Only $10.95+$1.95 postage & handling

Mail completed form to:

AXIOM INFORMATION RESOURCES P.O. Box 8015-T6 Ann Arbor, MI 48107 USA

MAKE CONTACT WITH THE STARS!

The **Celebrity Directory**™ **(9th Edition)** covers the entire spectrum of of celebrities. If a person is famous or worth locating, it's almost certain that their address can be found in the Celebrity Directory. ISBN 0-943213-31-2 **$39.95+$2.95 postage & handling.**

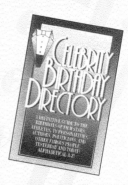

Use the **Celebrity Birthday Directory**™ **(4th Edition)** to find the birthdays of your favorite celebrities. Alphabetized for quick reference.
ISBN 0-943213-26-6
Only $10.95+$1.95 postage & handling

The **Celebrity Birthday Guide**™ **(4th Edition)** lists the birthdays of celebrities past and present. Thousands of entries by calendar date.
ISBN 0-943213-25-8
Only $10.95+$1.95 postage & handling.

The **1999-2000 Star Guide**™ is the most reliable and up-to-date guide available for over 3200 addresses of major stars from every field.
ISBN 0-943213-30-4
Only $12.95+$1.95 postage & handling.

Name_____

Address_____

City_____State_____Zip_____

____ Copies of **Celebrity Directory**™ @ $39.95 each + $2.95 P&H
____ Copies of **Celebrity Birthday Directory**™ @ $10.95 each + $1.95 P&H
____ Copies of **Star Guide**™ @ $12.95 each + $1.95 P&H
____ Copies of **Celebrity Birthday Guide**™ @ $10.95 each + $1.95 P&H
____ Copies of **The Marriage Book**™ @ $9.95 each + $1.95 P&H

Total Order $_____,_____

Star Guide-78¢
Celebrity Directory-$2.40
Celebrity Birthday Guide-66¢
Celebrity Birthday Directory-66¢

Total Postage & Handling $_____,_____

MI Residents add 6% Sales Tax * $_____,_____

Add $3.00 per item for 2nd DAY PRIORITY MAIL   Total Enclosed $_____,_____

The Marriage Book is a collection of words of wisdom every one should read before marrying.
ISBN 0-943213-26-6 LC#97-74584
Only $10.95+$1.95 postage & handling

Mail completed form to:
AXIOM INFORMATION RESOURCES P.O. Box 8015-T6 Ann Arbor, MI 48107 USA